101 Law School Personal Statements That Made a Difference

Dr. Nancy L. Nolan

Copyright 2012. All rights reserved. No part of this book may be reproduced or transmitted in any form or by any means, electronic or mechanical, including photocopying, recording or by any information storage and retrieval system without written permission from the author, except for the inclusion of brief quotations in a review.

Electronic and paperback versions published by:

Magnificent Milestones, Inc.
www.ivyleagueadmission.com

ISBN   9781933819624

Disclaimers:

(1) This book is a compilation of successful personal statements; it does not claim to be the definitive word on the subject of law school admission. The opinions expressed are the personal observations of the author based on her own experiences. They are not intended to prejudice any party. Accordingly, the author and publisher do not accept any liability or responsibility for any loss or damage that have been caused, or alleged to have been caused, through the use of information in this book.

(2) Admission to law school depends on several factors in addition to a candidate's personal statement (including GPA, LSAT scores and recommendation letters). The author and publisher cannot guarantee that any applicant will be admitted to any specific school or program if (s)he follows the information in this book.

Dedication

For students everywhere;
may the size of your dreams be exceeded only
by your tenacity to attain them.

Acknowledgements

I am deeply indebted to the students, professors, attorneys and admissions officers who have shared their perceptions and frustrations about personal statements. This book, which was written on your behalf, would not be nearly as powerful without your generous and insightful input.

I also want to thank my colleagues at www.ivyleagueadmission.com for providing a constant source of support, along with the best editorial help in the business.

101 Law School Personal Statements That Made a Difference

Table of Contents

Chapter 1: Introduction: The Law School Admission Process — 7

- The Role of Personal Statements in the Admissions Decision
- Writing Tips
- Common Pitfalls
- Strengths to Highlight

Chapter 2: Candidates with Legal Experience — 11

- Interest in Intellectual Property Law
- Active in Student Government
- Legal Work Experience
- Crime Victims & Witnesses

Chapter 3: Inspired by an Issue or Cause — 24

- Political Activists
- Current Event or Issue
- Feminists

Chapter 4: Inspired by Unique Life Experiences — 38

- Inspired by an Illness or Traumatic Experience
- Inspired by Religion
- Immigration & Travel

Chapter 5: Older and Non-Traditional Applicants — 50

- Scientists & Engineers
- Artists, Writers & Musicians
- Experience in Social Services
- Older Candidates
- Career Switch
- JD/MBA Applicants

Chapter 6: School-Specific Questions — 65

- An Ethical Dilemma
- Target a Specific School
- How You Will Contribute to the School's Diversity

Chapter 7: Addendums to Explain Unusual Situations — 77

- Disappointing Grades
- Low LSAT Score
- A Gap in Education or Experience
- Arrest / Criminal History
- Job Loss / Getting Fired

Chapter 8: A Second Chance: Responses to Waitlist Notices — 90

Chapter 9: Final Thoughts — 93

Chapter 1: Introduction: The Law School Admission Process

For most students, few processes are as daunting as applying to law school. Competition is fierce at top programs, which receive hundreds of applications for every seat in the class. Due to the large volume of applications that they receive, most schools evaluate candidates on a two-step basis:

1. **The Numbers**. The primary screening is strictly the "numbers" that reveal your intellectual strengths. To gain admission to a specific university, your GPA and LSAT scores *must* exceed the minimum cutoff level that the school has imposed. Selectivity varies greatly among programs, which means that scores that are considered "great" at one school may not be competitive at another. As a general rule, successful candidates at state schools have a minimum GPA of 3.0 to 3.5 (out of a possible 4.0) and a minimum LSAT score of 155 (out of a possible 180). At highly competitive programs, the cutoffs are as high as 3.75 and 170 for the GPA and LSAT, respectively. Candidates whose "numbers" fall below these levels can still gain admission in special circumstances, but their odds of success are greatly diminished.

2. **Personal Strengths**. Candidates whose "numbers" meet the school's expectations are further evaluated for their personal fit for their intended program. In the pre-interview stage, this "fit" is assessed from the applicant's personal statement and reference letters. Without exception, these documents *must* highlight the skills and traits that top schools covet, including honor, maturity, a solid work ethic and exemplary communication skills.

A great personal statement brings your "numbers" to life and provides a creative description of your performance and potential. It also provides critical information about your personality, ethics and integrity that isn't revealed anywhere elsewhere in your application. The BEST statements are short, specific and insightful. They are written by candidates who know what they want and aren't afraid to go for it.

Here is what the committee hopes to learn from your personal statement:

- Your unique qualifications, including the depth of your academic and extracurricular experiences
- Your personal traits and interests that aren't presented anywhere else in the application
- Your demonstrated commitment to pursuing a law degree – and why you chose it
- How you compare to other candidates with similar aspirations

An effective personal statement *supplements* the data you have provided the school about your academic and professional history, rather than simply restating or duplicating it. Ideally, it will provide the reader with critical information about your personality, ethics and integrity that they couldn't uncover any other way.

The Importance of the Personal Statement in the Admissions Decision

The most common question we are asked about personal statements is how they are used in the admissions process. As a general rule, they supplement the primary admissions criteria, which are your GPA and LSAT score. In highly competitive programs, the applicant pool can quickly be sorted into three categories:

a. candidates with excellent grades and test scores: good chance of admission
b. candidates who are borderline cases: application is competitive, but not outstanding
c. candidates with low grades and disappointing test scores: poor chance of admission

Unfortunately, if you fall into category c, even a great personal statement may not save you from rejection. In a highly competitive applicant pool, schools usually screen out lesser qualified applicants by imposing a minimum "cutoff" for GPA and LSAT scores. Although a personal statement can "explain" a disappointing academic performance, it usually cannot compensate for it. There are limits to how much leeway a school will give to a candidate who does not present a solid track record of success.

In contrast, essays from candidates in category a are usually disaster checks. These applicants have exceptional grades, top test scores and persuasive letters of recommendation. On paper, they are everything a top school is looking for. Their personal statements must:

- explain their motivation and goals
- document their character, integrity and work ethic

For candidates in category a (excellent grades and test scores), a bad or mediocre personal statement can be extremely harmful. In a highly competitive applicant pool, each piece of the admissions puzzle (GPA, LSAT score, personal statement, reference letters) must "fit" together in a cohesive manner to show the committee who you are and what you have to offer. If your statement is poorly written, or reveals a lack of focus and dedication, the committee will be less likely to take a chance on you.

Surprisingly, nearly 70% of the applicant pool falls into category b, or borderline. These candidates have competitive grades and test scores, but are otherwise not distinguishable from others with similar "numbers." Their acceptance or rejection often hinges on an exceptional intrinsic quality that captures the committee's interest and makes a positive impression. In some cases, this can be their commitment to family, their dedication to community service or their ability to overcome an obstacle. A persuasive personal statement that discusses a candidate's passion (and how (s)he plans to use that skill in the future) can make or break his/her application; it provides the final piece of the "puzzle" that the committee needs to become excited about the applicant.

Writing Tips

In a typical day, a law school admissions officer will read between 10 and 25 personal statements from candidates around the world. What makes a positive impression? Passion. Sincerity. Insight about yourself and the world around you.

From our experience, a great personal statement can take any number of forms; since no two candidates are alike, their personal statements won't be, either. Consequently, the only "magic formula" is honesty; you must have the courage to reveal your true personality, whatever that may be. Show the committee who you are and what you will bring to their program. Show them the contribution that only *you* can make.

We surveyed thirty admission officers on what they expect to see in law school personal statements. Here's what works:

1. **Answer the question that was asked**. Tell us why you want to become an attorney and why you believe you will be good at it. Show us that you have the maturity and insight to set and achieve realistic goals.

2. **Write naturally, but concisely**. Use simple sentences and your everyday vocabulary. Don't waste time on fancy introductions; get to the point quickly and reinforce it with specific examples.

3. **Use excellent grammar and punctuation**. Use logical paragraph breaks to separate your thoughts and to make the essay easier to read. Proofread your work carefully before you submit it. Don't let carelessness ruin your chances.

4. **Show your real personality (let us get to know you)**. Too many personal statements are long, boring theoretical pieces about politics, the economy or complex business issues. No matter how well-written or researched, they don't tell us a darn thing about the candidate. Anyone can write a rational, detached paper, but that's not what we are looking for. We want to get to know you and the unique contribution you will make to our school.

5. **Personalize your essay as much as possible**. Write about your own unique, funny, interesting experiences. Provide details to add color. Adopt a relaxed, conversational style.

6. **Use humor only if it works**. Few people can write humorous prose or recount funny experiences effectively. If you have this gift, by all means use it. Before sending us a "funny" essay, though, have several people read your material to make sure it comes across well on paper. Avoid anything off-color or mean-spirited.

7. **Convey a positive message (avoid cynicism)**. Many applicants discuss a misfortune they have experienced and how it has shaped their personality. Be very careful of your tone if you decide to write about a hard-luck story. Avoid the "victimization" perspective; instead, focus on how you *overcame* the setback. Show us how the experience helped you to demonstrate your stamina, perseverance and intelligence. If written well, these essays show us that you can succeed in the face of terrible obstacles. If written badly, they will make you sound plaintive, self-righteous and bitter.

8. **Use the active voice**. Nothing is more tedious than trying to read a personal statement that was written in the cold, detached passive voice. Although common in technical journals, it is pretentious and verbose in everyday writing. Keep your verbs simple and active. What's the difference?

Active Voice: The cow jumped over the moon.
Passive Voice: The moon was jumped over by the cow.

Yes, it sounds that silly when *you* use it, too!

9. **Explain events whenever appropriate**. The committee is interested in your accomplishments because of *why* you tackled them, what you thought about them and what you learned from the experience. Tell us the reasoning behind your decision and how your life changed as a result of it.

10. **Be specific and focused.** Rather than list several items or events, give a full description of just one. The more details you include, the more personal your statement will be.

11. **Proofread several times and get feedback from valued sources**. Explain to them what you hope to convey in your writing and ask them whether or not you met your objectives. The true test of your writing isn't what you *intended* to say, but what the reader actually understands.

12. **Revise and polish until it is perfect**. Give yourself enough time to do the statement well. Successful applicants usually invest several hours deciding the correct approach, constructing an outline and writing a first draft. You may have to write and revise multiple drafts before you are satisfied with your essay.

Common Pitfalls to Avoid

1. **Don't let anyone else tell you what to write**. Well-meaning parents and advisors often interfere in the writing process, which tends to sabotage the candidate's chances. Use your own best judgment in choosing a topic and writing your statement. Don't let anyone else influence you. We read thousands of essays each year, and have developed a keen eye for authenticity.

2. **Don't oversell yourself or try too hard**. Many candidates manage to squeeze every accomplishment they've ever had into a two-page personal statement. Others explain emphatically how much they "really, really" want to attend our school. Don't take such a desperate approach; just be yourself.

3. **Don't rehash information that can be found elsewhere in the application**. We already know your GPA, LSAT scores, academic awards and honors. Use your personal statement to discuss experiences that aren't revealed anywhere else. Consider your essay to be an informal interview, your exclusive "one-on-one" time with the committee. Show us why we should accept you into our academic community.

4. **Don't write a scholarly or technical paper on a specific legal case.** The personal statement is your only opportunity to demonstrate your non-academic strengths, particularly your personality. Don't waste it.

5. **Resist the urge to write a manipulative or argumentative essay on a controversial issue.** Be original. Each year, we receive hundreds of personal statements that discuss the horrors of nuclear proliferation and the dangers of global warming. Sadly, they don't tell us anything we don't already know. If you choose to discuss a meaningful issue, do so in the context of your demonstrated commitment to changing it, either through your career or volunteer work. Don't confuse passive idealism (or future intentions) with productive action. A demonstrated commitment to a cause is worth writing about; passive idealism is not.

6. **Don't try to explain blemishes on your record**. With rare exceptions, it is impossible to explain poor grades and test scores without sounding irresponsible or defensive. Neither will enhance your admissions chances. If you have a compelling excuse for an academic disappointment, place it in a separate addendum to your file, rather than in the body of your personal statement.

7. **Don't use large, pretentious words**. Use the simplest language to explain your meaning precisely. Using three-dollar words to impress the committee usually backfires, because it comes across as presumptuous and arrogant.

8. **Don't be boring and safe; tell a real story!** A fresh and well-written personal statement will enhance your credentials and aid your application effort.

9. **Don't lie or exaggerate.** Applicants seldom realize how easy it is to detect lies and half-truths in admissions essays. Don't pretend to be someone you are not. After reading your application, the committee will have an excellent "feel" for your character. Consequently, they will be able to sense if a reported event or achievement isn't consistent with the rest of your history. Lying is a fatal mistake. A single misrepresentation on your application will lead us to doubt all of your other assertions.

10. **Don't be gimmicky.** Avoid using definitions to begin your personal statement. This crutch was extremely popular in the late 90's, but is now synonymous with sloppy writing. Avoid using cute or "meaningful" quotations, unless they perfectly fit the character and tone of your essay. Quotations are terrific if they are seldom-quoted and deeply relevant to your chosen topic. All too often, though, their usage is cliche and the resulting essay is unimaginative.

11. **Don't play games with the word limit.** Don't use a miniscule type size or invisible border to shrink an essay to the stipulated length. Except in extreme circumstances, your finished statement should adhere to the maximum word limit. In many cases, less is more. Convey your points quickly and efficiently; don't feel obligated to "fill" extra space.

Strengths to Highlight

Your personal statement MUST emphasize the intrinsic traits that the committee seeks in the admissions process. Due to the high ethical standards and level of critical thinking that are expected in the legal profession, your character and motivation will be highly scrutinized by the selection committee. Use the essay set to sell your *whole* self, not just the individual pieces that you think the school wants to see.

Admissions officers seek the following traits in law school applicants:

Honesty	Creativity	Passion
Logical Thinking	Independence	Confidence
Humor	Perseverance	Communication Skills
Objectivity	Maturity	Strong Personal Ethics

To whatever extent possible, you should build your statement around the achievements and experiences that have enabled you to cultivate and display these strengths. This is your only chance to sell yourself; use it for everything that it's worth.

The personal statements of successful applicants will probably surprise you. They are seldom academic in nature, and may seem risky to candidates who feel compelled to assume a false (or misleading) persona for the committee's benefit. That's why studying these statements is so valuable. They reveal the heart and soul of each writer and demonstrate what (s)he would add to the law school class.

These candidates were accepted because they caught the eye (and captured the heart) of a receptive admissions officer. They have accomplished what you are trying to do. Before you sit down to write your own personal statement, read on!

Chapter 2: Candidates with Legal Experience

Many candidates have experience in the legal profession through summer jobs, volunteer positions, and relevant internships at private firms and government offices. Others have personal exposure to the profession because they have been victims of a crime or a witness for a civil or criminal case. Finally, some candidates are related to attorneys or interact with them through their work in another field; these experiences provide an extraordinary chance for them to observe the daily realities of the profession. For these candidates, the personal statement is a golden opportunity to explain how their exposure to the law has influenced their long-term goals.

Here are several excellent personal statements from candidates with legal experience who gained admission to highly competitive law schools. By design, we have grouped them into the following categories:

Interest in Intellectual Property Law
Active in Student Government
Legal Work Experience
Crime Victims & Witnesses

To protect the privacy of the writer, the names of all people, classes, schools, places, teams, activities, and companies have been changed.

Intellectual Property Law

By the time they left, the only item on my father's desk was the Snoopy calendar I had given him for Christmas. As the Director of Software Technology for Microsoft, he was one of the first people whose offices were searched during the Federal government's anti-trust suit against the global software giant. To a casual observer, the office looked like a tornado had blown through; Federal agents seized every piece of equipment, from disks and hard drives to fax machines and telephone cords. Although I was not there to witness the events, I was old enough to realize that life at Microsoft had changed forever. At age 12, I wondered how the fight over technology would affect my family's future.

In hindsight, my initial interest in the law arose from my personal fears; I wanted to be certain that my father kept his job and that what Microsoft did was legal. Surprisingly, when I began to ask questions about computer laws, I found precious little material. When I got my first computer in high school, I realized that advancing technology was opening doors that society and the law were ill-equipped to enter. This perception was confirmed by widespread anecdotes about computer failures during surgery, police arrests based on erroneous data, and devastating cases of identity theft and privacy invasion. During these years, the public finally began to confront and debate these dilemmas. As technology changed our lives, the law was forced to respond.

When I enrolled at MIT in 2005, the university did not offer a course that addressed the societal implications of advancing technology. During my sophomore year; Professor Edward James created and taught such a course for undergraduates. The class was a unique approach to education; we held roundtable discussions with guest speakers who were experts in this relatively young field, including technical leaders from Microsoft, Dell and Cisco Systems. We also invited speakers from the ACLU and the Computer Professionals for Social Responsibility to explain the consequences to the consumer. Through this class, I saw how well-intentioned laws can be misused against people, even by the government. I also witnessed how the absence of relevant laws can be devastating to both private citizens and technologically driven companies. Most importantly, I realized that constructing the law in response to a dilemma can be a slow and difficult process, particularly when the underlying issues are not fully understood. Nonetheless, I saw that I could use my problem-solving, reasoning, and writing skills to construct viable solutions.

Buoyed by the exhilaration of Dr. Edwards' class, I was eager to apply the same intellectual process to other societal problems. Consequently, I joined the model United Nations at MIT, where I researched, wrote papers, and moderated discussions on terrorism, economic unity and drug legalization. Our debates were sometimes more educational and practical than classroom learning, because they forced us to think outside the boundaries of academia. We acknowledged the need for negotiation and compromise, and we often constructed innovative solutions. More importantly, we participated in a rewarding process that identified and resolved societal dilemmas, much as our lawmakers do.

Every day, judges define how society will deal with complex issues, including the global implications of emerging technology. They contribute lasting improvements to society by addressing issues (like the Microsoft anti-trust case) that can potentially undermine its goals. I am applying to law school because I want to be prepared to participate in this exhilarating process. I want to play a meaningful role in litigating key issues that affect how technology will be used in the future.

Our Assessment: In this statement, this candidate explained his longstanding interest in technology law, which was rooted in his father's experience with the Microsoft anti-trust suit. Although long, the essay does an exceptional job of conveying the author's passion for the field – and his willingness to guide its direction. It was well perceived.

Interest in Intellectual Property Law

Even those who are comfortable with the Internet continue to think of it as the "wild west," a blazing frontier without rules, boundaries or quantifiable goals. When I joined Zenith Research in 2005 to build five-year forecasts of the online marketplace, my clients jokingly asked how I could possibly be held accountable for my predictions. At a time when the overheated economy measured job loyalty in months rather than years, few Internet analysts stuck around to explain the devastating "tech wreck" of 2007. Consequently, those who predicted a non-stop continuation of the Internet's explosive growth were rarely held accountable for their unrealistic projections.

In this respect, I am an anomaly. After an eight-month absence, I returned to Zenith Research in July 2009 to revise my earlier forecasts and to reconcile my previous expectations with the industry's current state. Although most of my original clients and colleagues had left the firm, I retained my sense of accountability. My post-mortem analysis has been both enlightening and humbling. I was encouraged by trends that evolved as I had expected, and disappointed to see where I went wrong. By analyzing my performance throughout a volatile marketplace, I improved my ability to predict trends and gained an appreciation of the evolving role of law and public policy in shaping the Internet's future.

Back in 2005, I drafted my initial forecasts using a classic business analysis: sifting though trade journals, interviewing industry executives and crunching alternative scenarios in Excel spreadsheets. A decade later, litigation and regulatory concerns are a higher priority than more conventional business issues. Anti-spam email legislation, FCC rulings on digital television and music industry lawsuits over online file-sharing carry more weight in my recent forecasts than once-critical marketing, technical and business strategy issues. Clearly, the Federal government has made several bold moves to define the limitations and guidelines of the Internet "frontier."

Like many of my peers, I am an idealistic supporter of the Internet's ability to provide accelerated global access to information and communication. My immediate reaction to the music industry's efforts to quash file-sharing was instinctive disapproval. Yet as an Internet researcher, I have come to understand the perspective of my clients in the music industry. Although we disagree about the industry's future, we have rationally discussed the merits of online music distribution, the consumer's willingness to pay for services, and the potential corporate benefits of file-sharing. Such dialogue makes it difficult to accept the stereotypical depiction of the music labels as villains, with Napster and its progeny playing Robin Hoods.

Increasingly, the high profile cases involving digital piracy tend to frame the debate in terms of right versus wrong, rather than what is best for consumers, companies and society-at-large. In many ways, the future of the Internet will be determined in the courtroom, as the legal system scrambles to regulate these unprecedented developments in technology. This intriguing situation inspires my application to law school, along with my desire to ascend to a leadership role in a twenty-first century Internet firm. Whatever the courts decide, I want to be well-positioned to preserve the medium's vast technological and creative possibilities.

New York University will provide a challenging environment for me to accomplish these goals. Because the Internet embraces so many areas---information technology, intellectual property rights, and global communications---NYU's breadth of faculty will bring a unique benefit to my studies. I am particularly intrigued by the proposed interdisciplinary research by Professors Davis and Hinkman, which will combine legal, industry and public interest perspectives on music piracy. With my experience at Zenith Research, I have much to offer this project and hope to contribute to its findings. As one of the few remaining Internet pioneers, I am committed to doing my part to research, analyze and influence the critical issues that affect its future.

Our Assessment: On a technical and creative basis, this essay is highly impressive. The author has a long and illustrious career in technology that he revealed to the reader through numerous observations and anecdotes. It is one of the most impressive statements about intellectual property law we have ever seen.

Interest in Intellectual Property Law

When I was eighteen, I enjoyed spirited discussions with my father about just about everything. One night, as we wrapped up a long debate about the merits of hybrid cars, he announced that I would make an excellent attorney. I was shocked. As an electrical engineer, my father had always encouraged me to pursue a technical career. Why would he suggest that I consider the law? When probed, he cited my natural ability to present a logical case during an argument. Long after my siblings gave up, I kept my composure and provided a valid counter argument. From his perspective, I was a natural.

Although I was intrigued by the idea, I opted to explore my passion for computer science at Boston University. During my first two years of college, becoming an attorney seemed as unlikely as playing third base for the Boston Red Sox. In my junior year, however, a class entitled "Technology and the Law" helped me to appreciate how the law touched several areas of my life. Most impressively, a subsequent class called "Computers and Law" revealed the importance of patent protection in the development of software, which is my chosen field.

Following my graduation in December of 2006, I accepted a position with Synergration, Inc., where I develop drug discovery software for the pharmaceutical and biotechnology industries. On a daily basis, the position allows me to flex my creative muscles by researching, evaluating and implementing new ideas. As I progress in the field, I am increasingly appreciative of the caveat from my "Technology and the Law" class; indeed, legal issues govern every stage of software development.

A decade ago, a technical firm could succeed simply by being the first to deliver a new type of software to the marketplace. Now, before a company invests a single dollar in product development, its intellectual property attorneys must ensure that the idea does not encroach on another firm's patented technology. Likewise, once a product is released, the firm must vigilantly protect its investment against competitors who want to enter the same market. Without patent protection, a company like Synergration would not invest the time, money or energy into developing new software. Our profits (and competitive survival) hinge upon the effectiveness of our top-notch legal team. If they fail to protect our intellectual property, the consequences to the company, employees and customers will be devastating.

The future of technology clearly depends on the careful delineation of rights and obligations regarding fair-business practices, regulation and jurisdiction, consumer rights and liability. I am eager to be a part of this evolution. As an intellectual property attorney, I will be well-positioned to ensure the individuality and global protection of both the developers and users of these emerging technologies.

As I prepare for law school, I often think back to my father's suggestion that I consider a legal career. At the time, I viewed my passion for technology and my "talent" for the law as mutually exclusive interests. I have subsequently discovered the fascinating interplay between these two fields and the need for talented professionals who embrace both. By fusing my technical expertise with a solid legal education, I can make a meaningful difference in the development and protection of emerging technologies.

Our Assessment: This author provides an eloquent explanation for his interest in intellectual property law, which is a natural evolution of his current career path. His early discussions with his father provided additional insight into his "powers of persuasion" that the committee would never have learned about any other way.

Student Government

I am passionate about protecting the environment. Unfortunately, my ranting and raving to my fellow students at election time about "civic duty" and corporate polluters often fell on deaf ears. I wanted people to get involved, but shouting at them didn't seem to be working.

When I returned to college in the fall of my junior year, my friend Devon suggested that we run a voter registration drive for the upcoming election. Our focus would be on environmental issues. During the previous summer, Devon had worked with an organization that lobbied to protect the indigenous wildlife in Utah, and he thought we could mount a similar campaign on campus. I was definitely interested.

Unimpressed by my typical "strong arm" tactics, Devon suggested that we spend more time providing information and less time heckling the apathetic bystanders. Admittedly, coming from a place of anger isn't as effective as rational thinking and sound logic. With Devon's support and direction, I was inspired. I spent the next two weeks researching all the candidates who were running in the election. This time, instead of focusing on those who safeguarded the environment, we used a bipartisan approach; we created a spreadsheet that displayed all of the candidates, their party affiliations, and where they stood on key environmental issues based on their voting history. We hung the sheets on billboards all over campus, which ensured that students would have adequate time to "research" their representatives in local, state and national government.

We also set up tables outside the Student Union that provided voter registration forms and information about the environment. This system worked very well; many students were interested in voting; now, they had concrete information to guide their decisions. Frequently, students would stop at our table and ask, "Which candidate are you with?" Although some were suspicious, many seemed impressed that we hadn't been hired by a congressional campaign or political party. Several people asked why we were doing this, and the truth was that it was because we cared about these issues.

By Election Day, Devon and I had registered hundreds of students who had never voted before. When the final numbers came in, we discovered that voter turnout on campus had increased by almost 20 percent, which was partially due to our efforts. Although my favorite candidate lost, I felt that I made a difference. More importantly, I channeled my passion for the environment in a manner that didn't strain my voice.... or my sanity.

Our Assessment: This author takes a lighthearted approach to a serious topic, which differentiated him from other student leaders whose statements were somewhat heavy-handed. Thankfully, he had sterling credentials on his resume and several recommendation letters that confirmed his contribution to campus life. As a result, this candidate's statement worked – it was an insightful complement to the other material in his application.

Student Government

When I became the President of the Iranian-American Student Association (IASA) at Columbia University, the organization had meager funding, a dwindling membership, and a bad reputation from years of incompetent leadership. My first initiative was to recruit a group of enthusiastic students to help renovate the group. By networking with local businesses and community organizations, we increased IASA's resources and became involved in volunteer activities in New York City, such as the Iranian Heritage Festival, New Year's Dance, and International Dinner Nights. Within a year, our membership increased by over 70%.

Our successful transformation of IASA did not come easily: I spent many sleepless nights posting flyers, writing scripts for cultural plays and soliciting potential sponsors. With the faithful trust and support of my fellow board members, I knew that IASA would have a powerful effect on Columbia's students and the New York City community. Ultimately, our work yielded tremendous personal rewards: IASA's first general body meeting attracted dozens of students who were eager to join our organization. I was honored by their presence and support.

My work for Students for Justice, a non-profit group on campus, sparked my passion for public interest law. Following the terrorist attacks of September 11, many students of Middle Eastern descent (including those who strongly support the United States) found themselves under a cloud of mistrust and suspicion. Sadly, few Americans truly understand our native culture or religion, which widened the gap between us. Students for Justice raises awareness of the difficulties that Middle Easterners face to adapt to the American culture. In addition to my work in New York City, I also conducted seminars in colleges in Boston and Newark, where many second generation Iranian-Americans and Iraqi-Americans are raised. In my travels, I documented the cultural and circumstantial distinctiveness of the two minority groups and assessed the bias against them by faculty, student government and local law enforcement.

Compared to major criminal trials and other national crises, issues about campus distress receive little public attention. Nevertheless, our society's indifference to these issues does not diminish their importance. By an overwhelming majority, Iranian-Americans who are educated in the US want to be accepted into mainstream society. We are eager to do our part to fight senseless acts of terrorism. Through the dedication of volunteers and leaders in the organization, Students for Justice has achieved several small victories in our quest for better communication and understanding. Each successful lecture and discussion that we organize raises awareness and brings us a step closer to our goal.

As a first generation Iranian-American, I appreciate the hardships that most immigrants face when they move to the US. Without money, language skills or knowledge of our legal system, few can understand or exercise their civil rights. My proficiency in Iranian and French enabled me to serve as a volunteer translator at the Jefferson Law Center, where I translated legal documents and petitions from Iranian immigrants. Because of my cultural and socioeconomic background, I communicated well with my clients and understood their concerns. As a public interest attorney, I will be an advocate for a group that currently lacks adequate legal representation.

Inspired by my ancestor's experiences in Iran, my honors thesis investigates an unprecedented legal event in Iranian history. During the US military invasion in 1968, children from Putma, Iran were sent into exile in a failed attempt to create communal unity. My research analyzes documents that were written exclusively in Iranian, including the eyewitness accounts of two individuals from different class backgrounds who lived in the same village during the movement. My goal is to assess the impact of the movement by examining the structure and organization of these exiled youth communities. By successfully analyzing historical documents from another nation, I have strengthened my ability to assess and document contemporary legal issues in America.

Since moving to the US at age 10, I have been committed to building a future that joins multicultural people in a spirit of tolerance and equality. My diverse experiences as an advocate have allowed me to cultivate the insight, perseverance and compassion that I will need to pursue a career in public interest law. With formal legal training, I will have the credentials and knowledge to establish a non-profit organization that benefits underprivileged youth. I am eager to apply my diverse skills to build a better future for my community.

Our Assessment: This statement, although long, documents the candidate's experience as an advocate and his motivation to pursue a career in public interest law. His honors thesis, which was subsequently published in a reputable journal, revealed his considerable skills as a writer, researcher, and social commentator. As a result, the candidate gained admission to several top tier programs.

Student Government

My mom likes to tell the story of when I was seven years old and announced my career plans to my Sunday school teacher. "I want to be a lawyer and the President of the United States." Unlike my classmates, who harbored more "traditional" dreams of being teachers, firefighters and astronauts, my commitment to a legal career remained unshakable. Whenever I watched trial recaps on *Court TV,* I was impressed by the attorneys' power to change lives by protecting their clients' rights. I quickly learned that a carefully crafted argument could break down seemingly insurmountable barriers.

In high school, I began to participate in legal proceedings as a mediator and in Mock Court. Through my experience on the Jefferson High School debate team, I learned how to think and act like an attorney. By drafting and defending arguments, I became adept at public speaking under stressful circumstances. I quickly learned how to develop a strategic advantage by preparing intelligent rebuttals to my opponent's arguments. By anticipating the merits of my adversary's position, I ultimately enhanced my own. Debating also nurtured my competitive spirit; long after my teammates withered in exhaustion, I remained invigorated. I simply had to win.

My communication skills were an asset at the University of Rhode Island, where I will complete my degree in Communications next spring. As the Senator of the Student Government Association, I lobbied at our state capital for increased funding for our university. I felt the scrutinizing gaze of the 50 distinguished legislators who had gathered for my speech. "Ladies and gentlemen of the Senate," I began, "Thank you for allowing me to speak to you today. I am a student at the University of Rhode Island, and I want to tell you why my fellow students and I deserve your support…"

As I lobbied for university funding, I began to understand the "inner-workings" of the political process and the complex factors that affect public education. Despite strong opposition, I was a persistent advocate for changes that would affect my fellow students. As the recipient of two prestigious awards (Student Senator of the Year and Outstanding Advocate), I cultivated the respect of policymakers on both sides of the issue. My fascination with the political process confirmed my interest in a career that would enable me to better influence policy development, implementation and revision.

Throughout my college years, I have worked as a community advocate in local organizations, including the Boys and Girls Clubs of Providence. During an internship in public affairs with the Rhode Island Chamber of Commerce, I developed a voter education television show and a website that focused on local elections. While working on the show, I concluded that a legal education is excellent preparation for public office. In addition to gaining a solid theoretical background, law students also develop the poise and stamina that are required to defend issues in highly charged, controversial settings.

My goal is to pursue a career in public interest law, as an advocate for non-profit organizations and other under-represented groups. To make positive changes in society, I need to augment my idealism with a solid legal education at XXX. With my background in public service, the school is an exceptional fit for my talents and goals. I am particularly eager to continue my advocacy work at the Children's Advocacy Institute and the Center for Public Interest Law. Since age seven, when I enthusiastically announced my intention to become an attorney, I have done everything possible to bring that dream to fruition. XXX is the next stop on my fulfilling (and challenging) professional journey.

Our Assessment: This candidate had exceptional recommendation letters that cited her strengths as a speaker and advocate. As a result, the committee was delighted to read about her early interest in the law and the methodical way that she prepared for this goal.

Student Leader (ROTC)

On a calm night in the spring of 200X, I stood watch on the bridge of the USS XXXXX in the Northern Persian Gulf. Things were considerably slower than the previous night, when our destroyers had launched numerous tomahawk cruise missiles into Iraq, which was 20 nautical miles to the northwest. During these slow nights on the bridge, when most of the crew was sleeping, I often took the time to contemplate my future. On this particular evening, I confirmed my decision to pursue a legal career.

Although I had always intended to go back to school after my five-year NROTC commitment, I had originally planned to study information technology. My interest in the field dates back to my childhood, when I decided there was nothing better than programming computer games for a living. Encouraged by my father, who has a doctorate in engineering, I completed four years of study in computer science at the University of Connecticut. Ironically, the further I explored the field, the more I realized that computers weren't all that interesting. Instead, I was far more intrigued by the legal battles that will ultimately determine the future of the software industry. To whet my appetite for the topic, in the final semester of my senior year, I completed a graduate level course called Technology and the Law. At last, I had finally found something I was passionate about.

Just before my graduation from the University of Connecticut, I questioned whether it would be feasible for me to attempt law school after a five-year stint as a naval officer. Assuming that it would take three years to earn my JD, along with a full year to complete the application process, I would be nine years behind my peers in terms of career development. When I voiced my concerns to my advisor, Professor Harold Winkler, he replied, "Sean, you're going to be 33 years old in nine years, regardless of your decision. Do you want to be 33 with a JD or without one?" I was sold.

So, why study law over computer science? Over the years, I have enjoyed several spirited scientific discussions with my sister, who is now a first year law student at the University of Georgia. Since we both have technical backgrounds, we constantly discuss the high profile legal cases that govern the computer industry: the Microsoft antitrust case, Napster's rights to share music files and the government's ongoing efforts to eliminate spam. Yet the greatest revelation from our discussions was an inherently personal one; I discovered that am more fascinated by the evolution of the law than the underlying issues in technology. Accordingly, while I stood on the bridge that night, I decided to forego further training in computers in favor of studying the law.

Unfortunately, my personal revelation brought forth a more practical problem; how was I going to prepare for a law degree when I was stationed halfway across the globe? Once I returned to my homeport at XXX, I completed a comprehensive preparatory course for the LSAT. Scheduling was a nightmare, because I was still working between 60 and 80 hours per week during a grueling maintenance period in the shipyard, followed by an equally intense training period. Additionally, I also went to sea for a week or two at a time, which made taking classes an even greater challenge. Since many classes conflicted with my work schedule, I actually taught myself many of the techniques behind the logical reasoning portion of the exam. My performance on the LSAT confirms the amount of material that I mastered in such a short period of time; in June of 2008, on my first try, I scored a 172 (which is in the top 5 percentile). Thanks to an aggressive, self-designed study program, I believe that I have acquired the requisite analytical strengths to succeed in a top-tier law program.

My motivation for acing the LSAT was two-fold: (1) to develop the reasoning skills that are necessary to succeed in law school, and (2) to prove that my undergraduate grades at UC do not reflect my current ability, character and level of discipline. Over the past several years, my experiences as a naval officer have given me a level of maturity and judgment that recent college graduates do not possess. At one point, I was accountable for the safe operation of a $5 billion state-of-the-art submarine. With 65 sailors under my command, I had to lead by example. I had to grow up. When I reflect upon my undergraduate career, I am amazed by how far I have come; my time in the Navy has forever changed my level of discipline and professionalism.

As a relative newcomer to the legal profession, I am open to several different specialty areas, including technology law. I am confident that my academic, personal and professional experiences have imbued me with a depth, maturity and motivation that your program demands. After reviewing my qualifications, I hope that you arrive at the same conclusions.

Our Assessment: This candidate brought a wealth of experience to the table, including several successful years as a Navy officer. In this statement, he explains his motivation for becoming an attorney, his painstaking preparation for the LSAT, and his hope for academic redemption after a disappointing early start at UC. His honesty, intelligence, and maturity came shining through, which earned him admission to several highly competitive programs.

Legal Experience - Social Services

"Innocent until proven guilty? Not when you are a minority kid from *this* side of town……"

As a volunteer at Second Chances, a non-profit legal-aid organization, I work with teenagers who have been accused or convicted of felonies. Our goals are to provide legal assistance for underprivileged teens and to raise awareness of the need for juvenile criminal rehabilitation. On several investigations, I interviewed teens in juvenile hall who had been deprived of objective examinations. Sadly, many children who committed minor crimes due to peer pressure faced sentences of 25 years to life.

While compiling a newsletter about noteworthy cases, I worked closely with two teens who were under indictment for serious crimes. During my interviews with their families and associates, I gained a deeper understanding of the legal system and a profound empathy for these troubled families. Their situations exemplified the inherent dilemma in any justice system: the law must simultaneously punish and protect these young citizens. Because they are receptive to new values and behavior patterns, juvenile offenders have the potential to reform and become positive contributors to society. Our goal should not be to condone teenage crime, but to prevent overly zealous punishment by creating a rehabilitation system that functions as intended.

Recently, representatives from Second Chances met with Congresswoman Camilla Sanchez to discuss the need to scrutinize and enforce the laws that pertain to underage criminals. She was particularly concerned by a case in which a 17-year-old boy (with no prior offenses) was sentenced to 25 years in prison for his alleged association with gangs. Our promising meeting with Congresswoman Sanchez raised my hopes for our flawed legal system. With the skills and commitment of trained advocates, justice is *always* worth fighting for.

Besides my work at Second Chances, I developed powerful leadership skills through my extracurricular activities. As the president of the Chinese-American Student Association at Stanford and the founder of the Sacramento Hip Hop Dance Team, I coordinated cultural and recreational events for thousands of people. By organizing our performances, delegating responsibilities and resolving conflicts, I maximized the efficiency of an organization with more than 100 members. I also became a strong leader and an excellent public speaker with a passion for motivating others.

Throughout my endeavors, my familiarity with the Chinese language and culture has provided invaluable opportunities for growth. As an intern for Universal Dialog (an international marketing firm), I translated business and marketing documents. I currently work as a volunteer translator for the Los Padres Law Center, where I translate petitions from Chinese immigrants fleeing China due to political oppression. In my work at Second Chances, my bicultural skills enhance my ability to relate to immigrant groups, particularly Chinese-Americans.

As I apply to law school, I am intrigued by the complex legal challenges relating to public interest law. My work at Second Chances has revealed the need for dedicated attorneys to work as advocates for minority and teen offenders. The legal profession offers a powerful opportunity for me to make a positive impact that mirrors my values, abilities and aspirations. With my help, every child will be fairly treated by the courts and regain a second chance for a productive and meaningful life.

Our Assessment: This essay gets bogged down with supporting details of the candidate's other activities in the fifth paragraph, which were highly important to her. Although the information was good, it diluted the impact of her original narrative about her work for Second Chances, which was well-written and persuasive.

Thankfully, the essay was short enough that the reader did not lose interest. But, to us, this is an example of what candidates do when they have the "option" of writing three double-spaced pages instead of two; they fill the space with "other" material that could easily have been presented in their recommendation letters. In this case, the candidate's discussion about Second Chances was so strong that the essay had a positive impact. She gained admission to her first choice school.

Legal Experience

The first time I considered becoming an attorney was in my Ancient History class in high school. As an American citizen, I was confused by Rome's previous state of "lawlessness." How could a community possibly exist without laws? And how could a single person wield enough power to bestow them on a large group? For the first time, I realized that the laws of American society were derived from the will of the people. This was a startling contrast to the situation in ancient Rome, where the laws evolved and changed on the whim of the monarch. Even at 16, I understood the dangers of such a situation, both to society as a whole and its individual members.

To explore my passion for the law, I majored in Political Science and Government at the University of Delaware. In my Criminal Law class, I learned how to use science to solve crime and create a credible chain of evidence. In addition to studying court proceedings and performing mock trials, I learned how to match fingerprints and determine the trajectory of a bullet. I particularly enjoyed the contemplative reasoning required to develop and present a case. Later, during my junior year, I took a course on children's advocacy. By reading excerpts of Supreme Court cases, I learned about the law in a more explicit way and became intrigued by its possibilities.

For the past two summers, I have worked as a paralegal in the office of David Stevens, who is an attorney with a private practice in Fort Myers, Florida. Although my duties were mainly clerical, I was exposed to a variety of cases and to the workings of a law office. The most interesting cases dealt with government regulations regarding intellectual property. One particular client, who wanted to market his software internationally, faced a complicated anti-trust battle regarding its "ownership." By learning more about relevant laws (and why they were written), I understood why the actions of Microsoft were considered (by some) as anti-competitive and why airline mergers were blocked because of anti-trust concerns. My work with Mr. Stevens provided an appreciation of the complexities of the law and how it relates to international businesses.

Aside from my academic and work-related experience, my personality is also an excellent fit for the legal profession. I love to debate controversial topics and am willing to argue against my beliefs to better understand my opponent's perspective. By understanding alternative points of view, I am better able to identify any logical flaws in an argument or position. This skill will undoubtedly serve me well in law school.

At Georgetown University School of Law, I hope to focus on business law, with a focus on antitrust and intellectual property issues. Thanks to my experience in David Stevens' office, I am intrigued by these areas and I want to help clients resolve them. Long after I learned about the legal system in ancient Rome, I continue to be fascinated by the law's influence on business and society. In an area as new and exciting as intellectual property development, I hope to develop and implement equitable rules to govern what is currently perceived as "lawless."

Our Assessment: Although not perfect, this statement explains the candidate's early interest in the law, which he continued to pursue as a student and paralegal. His background and skills were an excellent match for programs in intellectual property law.

Legal Experience

At first, it was just a lark. Later, it was more like playacting. I put on a slinky dress, flirted with a guy in a bar and got paid for informing his wife that he was, indeed, a liar and a cheat. For the past several years, I have pursued a successful career as a private investigator. Since 2006, I have held positions of increasing responsibility in civil and criminal law offices in Chicago, culminating in the establishment of my own firm, Morelli Investigations, Ltd. Through these experiences, I have learned how to organize, prepare and investigate cases in family law, criminal law, bankruptcy and personal injury claims. I also have developed an educated "sixth sense" about people and situations that "just don't add up."

In addition to my work experience, I also teach classes in criminal investigation at the Mundelein Police Academy. My classroom experience has provided valuable insights into the practical and administrative challenges of police investigations. I also became proficient with many spreadsheet, word processing, database and programming software applications that are used in contemporary law offices. Exposure to the inner workings of the State Attorney's office gave me an appreciation of the challenges that prosecutors face when they try to build a case.

Throughout my career, I have embraced every opportunity to maximize my contribution to the legal and investigative team. I have conducted research for individual cases, drafted motions and briefs, summarized transcripts and Shepardized cases. For high profile criminal cases, I have reviewed and sorted evidence and built compelling cases for acquittal. Few fields offer the challenges and satisfaction of preparing a legal case and seeing it argued successfully before a judge. The law is truly my passion.

My long-term goal is to run my own practice as a criminal defense attorney in Chicago. On a practical level, I have already cultivated my investigative skills and have built a solid reputation in the community. I am applying to the JD/MBA program for two reasons. First, I am eager to augment my practical experience with a solid foundation in the law. Second, I will also need to manage the administrative aspects of my practice, including the challenges of marketing my services and managing my employees. In such a highly competitive environment, I need to be as comfortable negotiating my fees as I am deposing a witness. Northwestern's JD/MBA program is highly regarded in the legal community because it provides this dual expertise.

With my unique background, I will be a great addition to your class. According to my clients and peers, I am smart, funny and driven. I will also bring a wealth of practical experience to class discussions that few other students can. I am eager to learn as much as possible from every person in the class, who has their own special story to tell. Most importantly, after graduation, my knowledge and expertise will remain in the community, as I build my successful private practice on Chicago's south side. After living, studying and working in the city for 30 years, I cannot imagine a better place to complete my education.

Our Assessment: This essay made a terrific impression because it was written in the author's own voice. By using simple sentences and an accessible style, she presented her credentials in a persuasive way. She also targeted a specific school that was an excellent match for her background and goals.

Exposure to the Legal System as a Witness or Crime Victim

One of the earliest films I watched with my father was *Trading Places,* which is a fish-out-of-water story about a homeless man and a Wall Street broker who exchange places for a few days. In several key scenes, my dad made astute observations about the stock exchange and the pitfalls of commodity trading. As the owner of his own successful hedge fund, he hoped that I would eventually share his love of the financial markets. No problem. Even at age six, I was captivated by the frenetic activity and profit potential from soybeans, winter wheat oil and pork bellies.

Following my graduation from Kansas State University, I enjoyed a successful career as a stockbroker. After receiving my series 7 and 63 licenses, I was promoted quickly into a regional management position with Madison Stockbrokers in Texas. By 26, I was the youngest manager of a New York Stock Exchange member firm. Under my direction, Madison's Dallas office became the most profitable branch in the US.

Following my success at the firm, I was confident that I had found a meaningful niche in the financial services field. My challenging position allowed me to develop my expertise in sales, marketing, research and management. After receiving additional licenses (series 4, 8, 24 and 65), I developed a reputation for being a knowledgeable financial manager. Ironically, my decision to accept a Vice Presidency with a rival firm (A.G. Edwards & Sons) in 2001 crystallized my interest in the legal profession. Unhappy about losing a key manager, Prudential sued me for leaving the company.

After surviving the initial shock of being sued, I found myself captivated by the legal process. As my case progressed, I was particularly intrigued by the complex challenges relating to securities law. Over the past decade, attorneys have struggled to keep abreast of the changes in securities regulations and the burgeoning increase in related litigation. This disparity has created a strong demand for attorneys who are fluent in NYSE and NASD laws. In my own case, I quickly discovered that lawyers on both sides lacked a firm grasp of the laws that governed my responsibilities as a stockbroker. I found myself explaining key concepts to them and assuming an educational role, rather than that of client or adversary. After settling the case in arbitration, I knew that I hadn't seen the last of a courtroom. A rewarding future lay ahead of me as a litigator.

My primary motivation for attending law school is to develop the expertise I will need to work in securities law. Combined with my managerial skills and my extensive knowledge of the financial world, a law degree will enable me to help individual and corporate clients resolve complex securities issues. As someone with executive experience at a top brokerage house, I can facilitate the discovery process and enable faster resolution to cases. I can also offer qualified legal advice about taxes, inheritances and other aspects of portfolio maintenance.

Throughout the years, my father's inspiration has provided a satisfying balance to my academic and professional commitments. My parents taught me to embrace intellectual challenges, particularly when the resulting knowledge will enrich the lives of others. Law school will enable me to assume a unique niche in the profession by helping a client base that is currently underserved. My managerial experience, academic strength and securities expertise will contribute to classroom diversity and to my eventual success as a litigator.

Our Assessment: This statement, although long, provides considerable detail about the candidate's background in finance. The information about the lawsuit was particularly memorable, because it gave him exposure to the "other side" of the legal profession. As a result, the committee understood the candidate's motivation to pursue a law degree at this stage of his career.

Exposure to the Legal System as a Witness or Crime Victim

As a child of two physicians (a heart surgeon and a neurologist), I never developed the invincibility complex that was common among my peers. Our family dinner conversations about unexpected deaths confirmed the cliché about living each day to the fullest. Like many over-achievers, I always had high expectations for my own performance and future. My college roommate once predicted, "You will do something great in life, like finding the cure for cancer or winning a Nobel Prize." Indeed, I always wanted to use my gifts to improve humanity, but I wasn't sure exactly how.

Ironically, the first lawyers I knew made my mother feel like a murderer. Despite her years as a compassionate caregiver, my mother was sued for wrongful death when a female neurological patient died quietly in her sleep. Although the circumstances were sketchy, the cause of death was ultimately determined to be narcotic overdose. Sadly, when the woman's husband mysteriously overdosed a few weeks later, their 9-year-old girl was orphaned.

As doctors, both of my parents lose patients to death, and neither is a stranger to the hurt, anger, and blame from grieving family members. Yet this case was different. When the attorneys filed the complaint on behalf of the daughter, my mother took it personally. She hated the fact that the system could punish her, despite her lifetime commitment to helping others. My mother was the same woman who received gift baskets and holiday cards from her loyal patients, who willingly attested to her competency and compassion. Yet little comforted my mother during the lawsuit, when she cried every day and was afraid to practice medicine. For a while, I hated "the system," too. If anyone had told us that I would eventually go to law school, I would have laughed, and my mother would have disowned me.

As the lawsuit progressed (and I matured), my perspective gradually changed. My mother's attorney, Zachariah Jones, worked vigilantly to defend her. His emotional counseling and legal expertise helped her survive the experience relatively unscathed. I admired his clever tactics and his ethical standards. As her attorney, Mr. Jones protected my mother the same way that a doctor protects his patients. I have always envied the powerful, trusting relationships that my parents have cultivated in their careers. When I met Zachariah Jones, I realized that I could achieve a similar connection with people in a legal career, by using my natural talents as a researcher and communicator.

During my undergraduate program in International Studies, I observed the powerful role of advocates in resolving global problems. Despite heavy protesting and State Department warnings, I worked for a summer in the World Bank's international community. The experience opened my eyes to the wide range of people, causes, and passions worth supporting on an international level. Our department headed the Development Marketplace, which is a venture capital fair for entrepreneurs from developing countries. Our program attracted compelling projects of exceptional need from around the world. Far from my comfortable life in the United States, I learned about the efforts to end female genital mutilation in Iraq and to establish micro credit in South America. I also acknowledged the dire financial problems and severe human rights violations throughout the world and the need for qualified advocates. Every person I met had a personal mission and overwhelming challenges that captured my admiration and support. I was incredibly proud to be part of a program that offered a chance for exceptional people to pursue their humanitarian goals.

This experience rekindled my fascination with international affairs, domestic security and the workings of our legal system. I returned to the United States determined to be an advocate for justice at the personal, community, national and international level. Whether they advocate for a patient's rights or international relief efforts, attorneys find resolutions for clients who are embroiled in personal and professional struggles. With my natural gifts as a communicator, I will fight effectively for the underprivileged and underrepresented majority. I will also provide a voice of reason in unjustified cases, such as my mother's, when a family's grief causes them to blame the wrong person. Throughout my life, my parents have encouraged me to follow my heart, regardless of where it would lead. After my rewarding experience at the World Bank, I am ready to pursue my legal education and make a unique contribution as an advocate.

Our Assessment: This author accomplishes something that few candidates do – she successfully combined two separate themes in the same essay. The first theme, which explained her mother's lawsuit, was memorable because it revealed her initial distrust of lawyers. The story about Mr. Jones confirmed that the candidate has a realistic perspective of what a compassionate attorney can do. More importantly, she also explained her own experience at the World Bank, which broadened her view of what she could ultimately accomplish with a law degree. The statement, although long, was well received.

Exposure to Legal System as a Witness or Crime Victim

Before my father's accident, I never realized how desensitized I was to the evening news. Each night, I sat through the steady recitation of car accidents, crime reports and personal mishaps as if they were plotlines in a novel. Since I didn't know the victims, nothing seemed real to me. Even in the saddest cases, I never stopped to think about the long-term effects on the person's family. Everything changed when it was my father's turn in the spotlight.

In the winter of 2003, my father, a fireman for the city of Milwaukee, was involved in a tragic accident. While extinguishing a brush fire on the outskirts of town, he discovered a flaw in his flame-retardant suit, which started to smolder in the intense heat. By the time he was able to undress, the suit had melted onto his skin, which left him with third-degree burns on nearly fifty percent of his body. During the week after the accident, my father was the lead story on most local news broadcasts, which decried the manufacturer for selling defective products. Yet, after the initial interest died down, the reporters moved onto the next story, which left my family to endure the months of agonizing recovery on our own.

Although we received a small financial settlement, it was not commensurate with the magnitude of my father's loss. In addition to his physical injuries, he also lost his ability to fight fires, which had been his lifelong vocation. Fortunately, my dad was not a quitter. Within a few months, he found a job as a security guard in an electrical plant nearby. This was a step down for a skilled firefighter, but the position was less physically demanding. Sadly, my father didn't have many options in the depressed Milwaukee economy, where employment opportunities were slim. But, to everyone's surprise, my father emerged victorious. He learned as much as he could about home and business security, and saw a niche for himself in this untapped market. A year and a half later, my father invested everything he owned into his own security firm, Davis Security Systems.

For the past ten years, my father, mother and I have all worked together at the small shop. With my knack for paperwork, I do everything from filing taxes, billing clients and keeping the books. In addition to serving as receptionist, my mother developed our ad campaign and implemented a successful marketing program. And my father continues to work sixteen-hour days soliciting business and providing the world class service that Davis Security Systems is built upon. Thanks to our collective efforts, the business has enjoyed increased profits each year.

Although people often tell my father that he is lucky, I disagree. There is nothing "lucky" about being the victim of negligence and being forced to start over at age fifty. Luck also played a miniscule role in building his business success, which is attributable chiefly to his grit and determination. Ironically, the same people often say that I am "lucky" to have attended Yale, one of the premier universities in the nation. They fail to see the extraordinary efforts required on every step of my educational journey.

When I first decided to apply to law school, I read an article in *USA Today* about the predictors of professional success. According to the author, who is a successful attorney, the number one determinant was whether or not a student's parents had completed college. I respectfully disagree. As someone who is "first generation college," I believe the more relevant criterion is whether the student is self-reliant. Although neither of my parents graduated from college, they are survivors. They recovered from my father's accident and built a successful business from scratch. They brought me into the business and showed me the importance of hard work in achieving any goal. Ultimately, their example has been more powerful and inspirational than if they had simply been "lucky." They taught me how to create my own luck.

Although few people in Milwaukee remember my father's accident, it was a defining moment in my life, which planted the seed for becoming an attorney. I want to help other families who have been victims of the many shoddy, dangerous products that are in the marketplace. Although I do not possess a country club pedigree, I bring something to the table that is far more valuable; I am from a family of survivors who refuse to give up. Whatever life throws my way, I will not fail.

Our Assessment: This candidate states his case simply, clearly and persuasively. By focusing on how his family survived the setback – and including specific details, he made a positive impression on the committee.

Exposure to Legal System as a Witness or Crime Victim

Three years later, I can barely type the word without hearing the devastating synonyms: fink, turncoat, traitor. No doubt about it, the public has mixed emotions about "whistleblowers." Even the word itself is pejorative; it conjures up an image of an irrational woman blowing a whistle like an alarmist. In my case, nothing could be further from the truth.

In 2001, I was in the midst of a satisfying career at the FBI when the 9/11 attacks occurred. Suddenly, without warning, everything was different. As the nation grieved, government agencies faced unprecedented scrutiny about the startling lapse in security. The questions, without exception, were completely legitimate. Why didn't FBI leaders do something when the Minneapolis bureau reported that Zacarias Moussaoui had signed up for flight lessons? Knowing his links to global terrorist groups, how had the US intelligence forces not "connected the dots" regarding his intentions? If FBI leadership had listened, could 9/11 have been prevented or minimized?

As the assistant to Colleen Rowley, a career attorney for the FBI, I spent nearly two years investigating and documenting our operations, which questioned our role in the 9/11 attacks. On a dark Friday afternoon in August of 2002, I proofread Ms. Rowley's summary memo to FBI director Robert Mueller, which outlined the agency's shortfalls.

At the time, I did not realize that document would become a critical part of history. In hindsight, it marked a watershed moment in the intelligence community, which culminated in Ms. Rowley's unforgettable testimony on Capitol Hill. Although many reporters criticized her words and her appearance, others lauded her act of courage; *Time* magazine named her Person of the Year for 2002, along with the whistleblowers from Enron and WorldCom. My former boss is now a legend and I am on my way to law school.

When I helped Ms. Rowley write the historic memo, I didn't realize that it would lead to countless hours of questioning by attorneys, lobbyists and citizens groups. I didn't realize that every word, thought and piece of punctuation would be held up to the highest level of scrutiny. This experience confirmed not only my decision to become an attorney, but my pride in being one of the so-called whistleblowers.

From the start, I supported Ms. Rowley's contention that the hierarchy at the FBI had skewed the story, rather than opt for full disclosure. This lack of integrity was a problem in an agency whose charge was to enforce the law. When I first joined the FBI, they stressed the importance of professionalism and integrity, both on and off duty. I understood our accountability to the American people, who entrusted us with their safety. The public had every right to hold us accountable for whatever lapses in security threatened their lives. Any efforts within the organization to close ranks and restrict the flow of information were counter to our mission.

Our statement mentioned some of the endemic problems at the FBI that required immediate rectification. Sadly, many current and retired agents decried Ms. Rowley's revelations to protect their own reputations. Yet in the aftermath of 9/11, the public's reaction was decidedly favorable; they admired Ms. Rowley for identifying the need for improvement. Her willingness to put the public's safety above her own professional advancement continues to be a profound inspiration to me.

Addressing the shortcomings in the FBI was bigger than any one person; it required changes at all levels of the organization. Fixing those problems is critical to every citizen of this country. In hindsight, I don't know if we could have prevented 9-11. Maybe, with improved information flow, we could have made it less than it was. Yet that really isn't the legacy of being a whistleblower. What I learned from the experience was to tell the truth. If you make a mistake, own up to it. When your ethics are challenged, follow your moral compass, which will lead you to the correct course of action. Even if everyone else is taking the path of least resistance, take the high road. Do the right thing. Lives could depend on it.

<u>Our Assessment</u>: This author had a memorable story to tell, which left a lasting impression on the committee. Her writing style, although simple, allowed her to present her ideas in a clear and orderly way. As confirmation, the candidate presented a recommendation letter from Ms. Rowley, which documented the applicant's contribution to the investigation. Her overall application was extremely strong.

Chapter 3: Inspired by an Issue or Cause

Many candidates use the personal statement to discuss an issue, cause, or personal experience that confirmed their desire to pursue a legal career. For the essay to be compelling, the issue must be something that you not only think about, but have taken the time to work on. For example, everyone (theoretically) opposes drunk driving, but few join advocacy groups such as Students Against Drunk Driving. Likewise, many people talk about improving the environment, but few participate in programs to clean the beach, recycle old goods, or organize fundraisers for green-related causes. In your personal statement, you need to demonstrate more than passive idealism; instead, you should discuss a problem that you cared enough to *solve*.

Second, do not ignore the most important aspect of the statement, which is to explain *why* this issue or experience is important to you. If you (or someone you know) suffered a loss because of an issue, how did it affect you – and how did you overcome that setback? What have you done to prevent similar obstacles in the future? If written honestly and intelligently, your statement can reveal a level of depth and insight that the committee would never learn about any other way.

A common sense caveat, however: if you choose to discuss a difficult experience, be sure to explain how you have learned and grown from it as a person. Your goal is not to elicit sympathy, but to position yourself as a survivor who has much to offer whatever law school accepts you.

Here are several personal statements about political and social issues from candidates who were admitted to law school. By design, we have grouped the essays in the following sub-categories:

Political Activists
Current Event or Issue
Feminism

To protect the privacy of the writer, the names of all people, classes, schools, places, teams, activities, and companies have been changed.

Political Activism

I first got involved in local politics in 2007, when I championed a write-in campaign to support Denise Shatner's election as the mayor of Boise. Just three weeks before the November election, I realized that none of the three candidates on the ballot were interested in representing the progressive values that I cherished. Rather than support someone with differing ideology, I decided to promote Denise. With just $5,000 in our pockets, my five-member team purchased buttons, window signs and door hangers to teach people how to vote for a write-in candidate. Our literature also explained the causes that Denise would champion, including the cleanup of toxic chemicals in Deere Lake and the construction of a homeless shelter in the Bayside section of Boise.

To our delight, Denise made it to a runoff election by beating a candidate who had spent millions of dollars and had battalions of paid staff. The energy boost was palpable. Around town, people who had never cared about politics were getting excited and young people who had just moved to the city came to the campaign headquarters to help. Most importantly, voters who had become cynical about the election process were starting to feel like they had a voice again.

My friends capitalized on this new excitement by organizing a voting registration drive, which I helped to coordinate. A quick review of the city's demographics revealed that many newcomers and young people were not registered to vote. For progressive politics, getting these folks registered was the first step to winning. By design, we didn't go to the usual campaign hot spots, such as supermarkets and street fairs; instead, we targeted more youthful hangouts. We hit the bars.

Every night, we went from table to table to talk about the campaign. As I registered people, I made new friends and caught up with a few old ones. Without exception, our message got a positive response; I explained why voting was important, why I supported my candidate, what the runoff was all about, and how people could get more information about the election. At the end of each night, we had a beer and shared our favorite stories of the night. I thoroughly enjoyed the chance to spread my candidate's message.

Denise lost the runoff, but was elected to the Board of Supervisors the following year as part of a progressive sweep in Boise politics. Rumor has it that the rousing success of 2008 was largely attributable to the residual excitement from our 2007 write-in campaign. I am honored to have made a contribution to the progressive efforts. Through the process of registering voters, I became passionate about mobilizing friends and strangers to vote their conscience. To me, this is what grassroots politics is all about.

Our Assessment: This light and breezy statement contained a lot of details in a relatively small amount of space. It also revealed the creative tactics the candidate used to get people passionate about politics. He is exactly the type of self-starter that the committee hoped to attract.

Political Activism

On Sept 13, 2001, I struggled with a miserable combination of shock and numbness after the attack on the World Trade Center. My pain for the victims was exacerbated by the sad realization that the United States was going to seek revenge for the terrorist attacks. Regardless of how or where we responded, thousands of innocent people, who had nothing to do with the attack, would lose their lives. The ramifications of this type of retribution were unthinkable to me.

I desperately wanted to stop the cycle of violence. At first, I considered writing to President Bush to urge him to use restraint and caution in response to the attacks. Upon further reflection, I realized that my letter would never make it through the bureaucratic filters at the White House. Still, the idea would not leave me, so I sat down at my computer and began to type the letter. In a moment of inspiration, the words flowed easily. An hour or so later, I mailed the letter to the White House, and, as an afterthought, I also emailed it to a few friends.

The response to my email was overwhelming; my friends and family members forwarded it to almost a thousand people around the world. Within a week, I began to receive positive letters from kindred souls in Europe, Africa and Asia, with whom my message of peace had struck a chord. I was astonished and gratified by the thoughtful responses to my letter.

One woman from China, Vivian Kim, asked if I would be willing to publish my letter as an ad in a major US newspaper. I agreed. Vivian, a global environmentalist and mother of three, is a true force of nature. Within a day of receiving my approval, she organized a group called the Peace Initiative and began to solicit donations to have my letter published in *USA Today*. When I learned that full-page ads can cost more than $200,000, I doubted that we would succeed. The sum seemed impossible to reach, but Vivian was determined and her supporters were ready for a challenge.

The Peace Initiative gained momentum with help from organizers in Japan, China, Great Britain, Germany, Brazil and the United States. Soon, we had a website and were in communication with Global Veterans for Peace, who were also counseling caution in our foreign policy and the need to understand the root causes of the WTC attack before we instigated more violence. Despite my doubts, with seemingly endless hours of work, the campaign moved forward and more money came in, mostly due to Vivian's tireless efforts.

To my delight, my letter was published as a full-page ad in the October 12, 2001, edition of *USA Today*. The public response was immediate and overwhelming. I received calls for interviews from numerous radio stations, newspapers and television reporters, which gave me more attention than I ever dreamed possible. For the next two months, I dedicated most of my time and energy to dealing with those responses. Since then, Vivian and her associates have moved forward with the Peace Initiative, and I am now a full member of Global Veterans for Peace. We continue to work for a peaceful world where all people are safe and have the basic necessities of life.

Our Assessment: This candidate is a devoted advocate who has led several initiatives to promote world peace. In this statement, he explains how he got started on that path by writing a simple letter to his friends after the 9/11 attacks. The story is strong, focused, and persuasive enough to make an exceptional personal statement. To strengthen his application, several community leaders wrote letters of recommendation on the candidate's behalf, which documented his accomplishments as an advocate. The resulting file was quite compelling.

Political Activism

When Dr. Clara White announced her candidacy for the Iowa Senate in 2002, few people took her seriously. After all, this former Iowa City mayor had been out of office for nearly two decades, while she raised her family and built a thriving pediatric practice. Nevertheless, several volunteers believed that Dr. White's name recognition was still something special. Since the district was Republican, the general election was not a threat. Our challenge was to win the nomination in the Republican primary against two fierce competitors. Again and again, we were told that it couldn't be done, that the city's political powers would line up behind someone else. We simply refused to hear that.

Sure enough, when the dust settled and the final candidates had filed for the senate seat, the political establishment had indeed coalesced around another candidate. An "insider" politician with ties to the city's special interest lobbies, he quickly amassed money and endorsements. He also hired the city's most feared consulting firm to run his political campaign, which saturated the district with direct mail ads and commercials on cable television. Our opponent spent $350,000 on the race, compared to our $17,000. And we won!

Dr. White's campaign was a model for cheap and efficient advertising. While our opponent ran commercials and racked up endorsements, we stuck with yard signs that featured a silhouette of our candidate and the word "integrity." For the older citizens in our community, Dr. White's signs brought back memories of her years as mayor, before the city fell into the grasp of the special interests and political consultants. Our single direct mail piece also stressed the integrity theme.

In October, we finally received our big break - the city's daily newspaper, the *Iowa Star*, endorsed Dr. White. According to the political editor, her campaign theme of integrity defined the underlying issues in the election. Our leading opponent had lined up powerful special interests, but his own past was suspect; not only was he having tax problems, but he had even done time in jail for failure to pay child support.

My job was to promote Dr. White's candidacy throughout the community. I distributed literature, wrote press releases, and put yard signs on every corner in city. I also knocked on doors, recruited volunteers, and tried to create a presence in parts of the district where our candidate was less well known. For several weeks, I used every low-cost method I could find to stress a simple message; our candidate has integrity and she's back in politics.

On Election Day, Dr. White pulled off a stunning upset, winning 53 percent to 31 percent, with 16 percent going to the third candidate. To everyone's amazement, grassroots politics had defeated the money, the special interests and the endorsements. In Iowa, it's the new American way.

Our Assessment: This is a great essay that highlights the candidate's work on a special election for a dark horse candidate in Iowa. In some places, the writing could be sharper, but the underlying message is clear. This is a dedicated candidate with a passion for politics and sophisticated marketing skills. He was a great fit for the programs that accepted him.

Political Activism

As a veterinarian at the Rocky Mountain National Park, I have worked with the Denali wolves since 2008. Thanks to the efforts of the staff, the wolves have quietly entertained and enthralled hundreds of thousands of visitors each year. They are remarkably accepting of humans at close distances, which is unique among wild animals. However, during the winter of 2009, the pack left the safety of the park on hunting forays, where they were routinely trapped and killed. In January of 2010, the entire Denali pack was ravaged by trappers near the park entrance, leaving only two survivors. Luckily, the two were an alpha male and alpha female, who mated and had pups the following year. Despite their miraculous survival, the future of the pack clearly hinges on the protective interests of concerned humans.

In late 2010, my friends at the Colorado Wildlife Alliance submitted a proposal to the United States Board of Game to create a no-kill "buffer zone" adjacent to the park, which would cover the areas where the wolves are known to frequent. Although more than 80% of the state population supports wildlife, the Board of Game was composed entirely of hunters and trappers, who opposed additional hunting restrictions. Despite these terrible odds, I was committed to protecting the packs.

A week before the meeting, I created a simple website that summarized the issue, including photos that showed why the wolves deserved special protection. I also established a petition on www.thepetitionsite.com, which asked visitors to write personalized letters to support our cause. Clearly, with only a week's time, I had to aggressively promote the site. I started by e-mailing everyone in my address book, along with every environmental group I could find in Colorado. Next, I wrote a short press release that our local newspaper agreed to publish. Finally, I drafted a letter to the editor of every newspaper in Colorado, which included the URL of the website.

To my surprise, almost 6,000 people signed our petition, including wildlife lovers from every state in the union and more than 26 countries. The night of the Board of Game meeting, I decided to stage a media stunt to leverage the overwhelming support. I loaded several boxes of signed petitions onto a truck and asked local news reporters to film me carrying them into the meeting. We made the six o'clock news, and the petition helped to convince the Board of Game to create the buffer zone. Thanks to all of the wonderful people who supported the cause, the Denali wolves will be able to entertain a new generation of wildlife enthusiasts in a protected yet nurturing environment.

Our Assessment: This candidate is a seasoned veterinarian with a passion for wildlife and animal rights issues. Her recommendation letters documented her commitment to numerous causes in these areas, which made her a reluctant media star in Colorado. In this essay, she focuses on a single initiative to save the Denali wolves, which caught the attention of animal lovers from around the world. The essay – and the candidate – was well perceived.

Political Activism

As a third-generation descendant of the Chippewa tribe, I was raised with a starling lack of information about my family history. A divorce in my mother's family, along with stories of abuse and alcoholism, caused an estrangement in 1948 that continues to this day. Although my mother is curious about her ancestry, she respects my grandmother's wishes to "let sleeping dogs lie." If only I shared her complacency.

From the moment I looked in the mirror, I was fascinated by the physical features that distinguished me from my Caucasian friends. My brown skin, long black hair, and almond eyes suggest that my mother's ancestors, like those of my father, were full-blooded Kansas Chippewa. As such, they most likely were ranchers who endured harsh winters on the prairie simply to feed their families. Was it from them, I wondered, that I inherited my love of farming? Is my ability to shoot a rifle because of my training or something in my blood? More importantly, was I wrong to maintain my connection to the land, despite its limited financial potential?

Until I enrolled in college, I did not explore my questions about my family history. At the University of Kansas, however, I decided to attend the annual Native American Cultural Festival, which attracted hundreds of people from across the nation. While strolling from booth to booth, I encountered a small group of women who were gathered in a silent prayer. To my surprise, one of them smiled, held out her hand, and asked me to join them. It was my first tentative step to discovering more about my Native American culture. Through a series of classes in history and government, I have embraced all aspects of the Chippewa tribe. In doing so, I have debunked several myths that dominated my childhood impressions.

Oddly enough, Native American history has traditionally been taught from the Caucasian perspective, which depicts the Chippewa as passive victims in their own destruction. In my college classes, I was proud to learn that my ancestors were much more clever and proactive than historians were willing to admit. My investigation into this area comprised my senior thesis, which received the University of Kansas Award for Excellence in American History, the highest academic honor for undergraduate research.

To honor my heritage, I joined the Native American Conservancy Board (NACB) to petition and lobby the Federal government to preserve the rights of Native Americans on Kansas reservations. Rather than "develop" the land for use as casinos or shopping malls, I urged the government to retain the land for its original use to feed and nurture the indigenous families that still lived there. From my perspective, "development" was a thinly disguised excuse for evicting Native Americans from their homes for the benefit of private industry. With little fear of economic reprisal, corporations viewed the faltering reservations as easy pickings for their nefarious goals. Sadly, most Americans agreed that their efforts constituted "progress."

Although the NACB did not prevent the development, the experience introduced me to politics. Frustrated by our failure, I assumed the presidency of the NACB in 2009 and aggressively promoted our agenda. For the past two summers, I have attended several conferences regarding Native American issues and have published my findings in the *Journal of Native American History*. To my dismay, I discovered that the

American government continues to be shameful in its treatment of Native Americans. Whenever the Federal government extends a hand, it simultaneously turns its back, which allows state governments to chip away at Native American autonomy. My anger at the sad state of Native American affairs is the source of my interest in the law.

For meaningful changes to occur in Native American society, we need many things, including the dedication of good lawyers. So I aim to become one. In retrospect, I have followed a long, odd road to reach this point, beginning with my curiosity about a feud on my mother's side of the family. Who would have thought that getting the answers to a few questions would have led to something this extraordinary?

<u>Our Assessment</u>: This essay describes the candidate's journey to unravel her family's history, which ultimately fueled her passion to preserve the rights of other Native Americans. Although it is somewhat long, it is an honest, focused, and persuasive essay that reveals the many positive traits the candidate will bring to law school. Her leadership experience with the NACB, along with her accomplishments as a writer and researcher, was particularly well perceived.

Political Activism

As an award-winning journalist, my father has written for the *New York Times* for 38 years. Consequently, my siblings and I have always held a healthy respect for freedom of speech and expression. From my earliest memory, my parents taught us to view issues with a critical eye and to analyze news reports for their content, rather than sentiment. As a journalism student in college, I took those lessons seriously.

The events of September 11, 2001 tested my ability to view the news objectively. Although the media had always bombarded us with graphic images of suffering, this was different. My city was on fire and my friends and neighbors literally ran for their lives. In a split second, I lost every gram of desensitization that my father had instilled in me. Like many people in the United States, I was glued to my television for weeks, watching commentators try to make sense of the devastating events. After seeing the bloody massacre re-played over and over again, I went to bed with a deep sense of foreboding about the future.

At the dinner table every evening, my father and I discussed what I had seen on television and why I was so sad and terrified. To my surprise, he did not share my fear and anxiety. When he ended our conversation one night, my father advised, "Read more than you watch." Rather than catch the morning news on television, he suggested that I read the *New York Times*. Unlike the visual reports, which were filled with emotional images and touching music, the paper offered a more objective source of information. It was my choice, he said, whether or not I lost sight of the truth in the story. If I continued to rely on the emotional "spin" of network news, I would give the gruesome pictures too much power. In his mind, the words told the *real* story.

My father was right. After that last sleep-deprived evening, I started to read local and national newspapers to put the events in their proper social and historical context. Rather than limit my perspective to that of mainstream journalists, I also scoured the literature for essays that were written by theologians, teachers and scientists. Whenever possible, I ignored their graphic images to ensure that I focused on the information, rather than my own emotions. Over time, my critical eye became more focused when I sat down to read. Eventually, I was able to put the terrorist attacks into perspective. America was down, but not beaten; with time, energy and healing, we would recover.

Within a few weeks, as my father predicted, I began to sleep better. I had re-claimed my power in a situation that left the rest of the world feeling powerless. Fortunately, as I read about opportunities for participation and service, I found a positive outlet for my creative energy. Rather than view myself as a victim, I began to see myself as a force for change. As the Columbia University chairperson of the 9/11 Relief Mission, I led a student organization that promoted peace through tolerance and education. I also met several impassioned advocates who conducted groundbreaking research for the 9/11 Commission. Their determination to investigate and reveal the truth was a true inspiration to me.

Although I regained my sense of journalistic objectivity, I did not abandon the raw emotion that accompanied the devastating loss of 9/11. I am still deeply saddened by the images of suffering I have seen in nations across the globe, which have been the victims of similar terrorist attacks. I have learned, however, that the real story is not in the pictures, but the details. We only heal when we absorb the hope and truth of a situation, not when we wallow in emotion. Information is power, which makes it the strongest tool in a journalist's arsenal. Like my father, I am committed to using my power appropriately, by disseminating quality information with the highest standards of integrity and skill.

Our Assessment: This statement, although somewhat repetitive at the end, is unusually honest and thoughtful. From the committee's perspective, it was fascinating to read the advice that the candidate received from her father, who is an award-winning journalist. Ultimately, the candidate used that advice to resolve her issues with 9/11 and to confirm her own passion for journalism.

Political Activism / Started a Non-Profit Group

As a child, I always dreamed of being a "business woman" in New York City. Although I knew that only a tiny percentage of hopefuls could succeed in the Big Apple, I was sure that I would fulfill my dream. After all, I come from a family of survivors. During my last two years of college, my dad endured severe complications from diabetes, which he developed at 37. To pay for my college tuition, I worked a full-time job as a cocktail waitress, in addition to my heavy course load. Unfortunately, my father's disease did not respond to aggressive treatment methods. When hyperbaric therapy failed to eliminate the infections in his right foot, he decided on below-the-knee amputation. As a result, I spent a significant part of my junior and senior years of college teaching my dad how to walk again.

When we ventured outside, I saw the world differently – and felt the discouragement of a handicapped person firsthand. Wheelchair ramps were a rarity, and discourtesy towards people with disabilities was unfortunately common. In my anger, I wondered why the laws were not protecting my dad. Why were so many companies exempt from the Americans with Disabilities Act? Without the cooperation of government and business, my father's new world was not a hospitable one.

Immediately after college, I left for New York City with my dad's blessing. Despite his hardships, he was adamant that his medical condition not interfere with my professional dreams. At the time, I tackled my media career with the raw energy, focus and passion that were essential to succeed in New York City. My goal, beyond making my parents proud, was being "successful" in monetary terms. Thanks to the support of my family, I knew that could tackle any obstacle that came my way.

Ironically, before my father's amputation, I had never given much thought to discrimination in the workplace. Within a few years, however, I had two significant experiences in which male colleagues with appreciably less experience and revenue productivity were awarded promotions ahead of me. The first time, my dad encouraged me to discuss my concerns with my supervisor. Amazingly, he told me that I did not "need" a larger salary because I was a single woman who was "fortunate" to earn what I did. Not surprisingly, the colleague who got the promotion was my age, but had two children and a stay-at-home wife – a lifestyle choice that was identical to that of my male publisher. The second career incident closely mirrored the first, except that I discussed the scenario with my human resources department instead of my direct supervisor. Two days later, I was offered a 25% salary increase, but I resigned shortly thereafter. When I happily declined the significant counter-offer, which included a non-disclosure agreement, I came to a profound realization. Being successful was not measured strictly by monetary terms; it now included values and standards that I refused to compromise.

After my bouts with employment discrimination, I became zealous about knowing and protecting my rights. When I studied the Federal and State employment laws, I discovered that New York had some of the weakest employee rights in the country – so much for my childhood fantasies of the Big Apple! Determined to help younger women with less seniority, I formed Equality Now, a professional organization that promotes equality in the workplace. During my five-year leadership of the group, I gave numerous speeches on behalf of gender equality, including the keynote speech at the 2009 Governor's Ball. My goal, as always, was to empower other women to challenge themselves to realize the value that they brought to the workplace.

Through my work with Equality Now, I realized that success has nothing to do with money, but comes from a deep and honest commitment to make the world a better place. After careful introspection, I have realized that I can make the greatest difference in the world by becoming a lawyer and providing a voice for people and issues that would not otherwise be heard. After watching my father's struggle, I want to do my part to make the world a more hospitable place for victims of discrimination. As Mahatma Gandhi advised, I will create the change that I desperately want to see.

Our Assessment: This essay, although long, reveals the candidate's work as an advocate and her passion for victim's rights. She was the perfect match for the program in public interest law in which she ultimately enrolled.

Inspired by a Current Event or Issue   - The Achievement Gap

For my research project in my Education and Politics class, I investigated the impact of the "achievement gap," which costs the U.S. between $350 and $425 billion dollars in GDP each year. The largest contributors to this gap are minority children, who currently comprise nearly 45% of our school-age population. As a first-generation college student who was raised in an Arabic-speaking household, I understand the challenges these students face to succeed in a foreign educational system. Without positive mentorship and support, the achievement gap can be nearly impossible to bridge.

When I researched this dilemma, I was determined to find a viable way to narrow the gap in my own community. In 2009, I launched a non-profit organization called A World Without Limits (AWWL), which provides academic mentorship to the students who need it the most. On a theoretical basis, the goal of AWWL is to give all children, regardless of their race or socioeconomic status, an equal opportunity to succeed in the classroom. On a practical basis, I also hoped to provide poor and minority children with academic resources that are beyond the reach of their inner city schools.

Through one-on-one coaching, AWWL empowers students to realize their intellectual capacity and pursue their college aspirations. Historically, inner-city students from low-income communities have under-performed on most standardized exams, which limits their access to the most prestigious college preparatory programs. In many communities, this type of academic segregation begins as early as middle school. AWWL aims to level the playing field by providing inner-city students with an academically-focused culture that offers them adequate time to master the skills they will need to qualify for top programs. We also provide positive mentorship and role-modeling to help students appreciate the opportunities that they will enjoy if they continue to excel in school.

By design, A World Without Limits promotes the virtues of perseverance, higher education and intellectual curiosity in all of its participants. When they join the program, each student is matched with a college student who has enjoyed a successful academic career. Through meetings and tutoring sessions, the mentors share their advice about the educational process. By doing so, they provide the students with a critical support structure that is rarely available in inner-city schools, which lack the financial resources for outside programs and role-modeling. AWWL fills this void by emulating the strengths of non-profit organizations such as Teach for America and REACH, which maximize our ability to provide meaningful academic opportunity in poor communities.

After a successful two years, I am excited about the many ways that AWWL can expand its reach and make a lasting impact on the communities we serve. With the support of my faculty and peers, I believe that it has the capacity to provide meaningful, cost-effective educational intervention in hundreds (and perhaps thousands) of inner-city classrooms. Eventually, organizations such as AWWL can narrow the achievement gap and change the lives of millions of youths in the United States, who have the ability and desire to transform their dreams into reality. I am thrilled to do my part to guide the way.

Our Assessment: This candidate used the same essay to apply for several service-related scholarships. From an admissions perspective, it showed his passion and initiative. On his own, the candidate identified a problem and took the initiative to try to solve it in his own community. This is exactly the type of creativity and independent thinking that top law schools are looking for.

Inspired by a Current Event or Issue - Health Care

The continuous economic growth in Bahrain, which has been fueled primarily by the oil and real estate industries, has made a great improvement in the nation's standard of living. However, the nation's health care system remains substandard and unreliable. Despite a population of nearly three million people, Bahrain only has a handful of small hospitals. Few of them receive funding from the federal government, which limits the technological advancements they can offer their patients. There is also a dire lack of training, licensing, and regulations for the health care professionals who are responsible for treating and diagnosing a wide range of illnesses and injuries. As a result, thousands of patients die in Bahrain every day because of improper medical care.

An additional complication is the misplaced priorities in health care. In Bahrain, the system is governed by money, rather than ethics. Regardless of the severity of the case, patients who have money are always treated first. Those who do not have money are unlikely to be treated at all. In April of 2011, my two cousins got into an auto accident while visiting our extended family in Bahrain. Yan's foot was severely crushed, which required immediate medical treatment. Lee rushed her to the nearest hospital, where she hoped that Yan would receive proper care and compassion. Sadly, the doctors refused to treat Yan until the hospital received $3,000 USD. To obtain this amount of money, Lee had to leave Yan alone at the hospital for several hours while she waited for treatment. If she had not returned with the required fee, Yan would likely have died in the waiting room.

Ironically, wealthy and insured patients also struggle to obtain quality care. Last winter, my grandfather was hospitalized in Bahrain with severe abdominal pain. The facility that admitted him had the highest standards of care in the nation. During the first week, my grandfather's doctors prescribed medication for irritable bowel syndrome, which they insisted was the source of his pain. Unfortunately, his condition continued to deteriorate. Nevertheless, the doctors sent my grandfather home with a stronger medication and told him to "have faith" in their diagnostic skills. The cost for his hospital stay, in which his condition only got worse, was $30,000 USD. A week later, when he returned to the U.S., my grandfather sought treatment for the same symptoms at a public hospital in New York City. Within a day, the doctors determined that he had a carcinoid tumor in his colon, which was the source of his discomfort. My grandfather's condition improved greatly after its removal. Sadly, his case, which is far from unique, reveals the poor training and unethical practices of health care professionals in Bahrain.

Because of the high cost and unreliable reputations of many doctors, the people in Bahrain often buy their medication directly from the pharmacy, where all drugs are available without a prescription. Sadly, the pharmaceutical industry is not well regulated in Bahrain, which makes this approach inherently risky. Although the law requires that all pharmacies have a government license, many owners obtain them by bribing local officials or falsifying their application documents. Then, these unqualified owners engage in deceptive practices to increase their profits, such as diluting the drugs and changing the expiration date in order to sell old medication. There is also a knowledge gap, which prevents the average citizen from choosing the correct drug and dosage for their particular illness. As a result, people often exacerbate their problem by choosing the wrong drug, taking it incorrectly, and ignoring potentially deadly side effects and drug interactions.

Although the public is well aware of these issues, the federal government continues to ignore them. If they invested money in the health care system and enforced strict regulations on the standards for care, medication, and the training of health care professionals, considerable pain, suffering, and loss could easily be prevented.

Our Assessment: This is a serious, well written, and well documented statement about an important issue in the author's native country. Because she was applying to a highly competitive program with a focus on public interest law, it was also a highly relevant (and somewhat unusual) topic for the admissions committee. By adding the personal anecdotes about her cousins and grandfather, the candidate gave this essay the detail it needed to be persuasive and memorable.

Inspired by a Current Event or Issue - Children's Rights in Divorce

As she turned to leave the room, eight-year-old Erica raised her arms for one last hug. "I love you, Sara. Thank you for listening." My heart burst with happiness as I watched my young playmate jump into her mother's car to go home. As a volunteer for Kids United, where I work with troubled children, I was honored to play a role in making Erica's world "right" again.

As the child of two physicians, I was raised with a powerful desire to serve others. Unlike my parents, however, my passion is not medicine, but the legal and sociological aspects of family life. Like many children of divorce, I grew up with many unanswerable questions about what it means to be a family. Despite my parents' earnest explanations, at age six, I was simply too young to understand why my father no longer lived with us. My lifelong efforts to cultivate positive relationships within a fractured family have not only made me a stronger person, but inspired me to help others who are struggling with similar situations.

As a high school freshman, I accompanied my mother on a humanitarian trip to Guatemala, where she provided medical care to poor and underserved communities. After helping her in the clinic each day, I was delighted to provide an empathetic ear to the local children. In this impoverished environment, in which food and medicine were luxuries, my own problems seemed selfish and immature. I was privileged to become part of the children's lives, if only for a short period of time. As I listened to their stories of real human suffering, I was compelled to make a difference. By the time I came home, I had acknowledged my calling to provide emotional support and encouragement to children in disadvantaged situations. Throughout high school and college, I have volunteered at Kids United, where I counsel children who have academic and social problems. By working closely with third graders like Erica, who need the benefits of personalized counseling, I help them to develop good study habits and to handle their problems at home. I have also confirmed my desire to specialize in family law, so that I can make a meaningful difference in my clients' lives.

As a child, I did not understand the concept of "sole custody" in a divorce decree; now, I am aware of the ramifications of this decision on the daily lives of every family member. Many children are defeated by their parents' divorce, because their needs are not addressed. As an attorney, I can help to ensure a better future for children whose lives have been disrupted by divorce and abuse. I want to provide a voice for those who did not cause the discord, but are most directly affected by its implications.

Our Assessment: The personal details in this essay explained the candidate's motivation to pursue a career in family law; the opening anecdote about working with children was particularly well perceived.

Feminism

Although my mother calls me a dreamer, I prefer to see myself as an agent of social change. Perhaps naively, I believe that if enough people on this earth champion a cause, we can reverse our downward spiral of poverty, depression and despair. Caring is just the first step, however. People must act on their ideals by working together to achieve the social reforms that are necessary for our collective survival. After examining the many worthy causes in need of support, I have opted to focus my energy in the reform of feminism.

Why feminism? The obvious answer is because I am a woman, which makes me keenly aware of the subtle forms of discrimination that continue to plague my sex. Another reason is my deep-rooted sense of justice, which inspires me to fight on behalf of those who are placed at an unfair disadvantage. But the primary reason is that I am courageous enough to handle the many challenges and obstacles that being a feminist presents. Every cause needs a champion who is fearless; thankfully, the feminist movement has me.

Inspired by a personal meeting with Gloria Steinem, I decided to start a young feminist club at John F. Kennedy High School to address issues regarding gender equality. We organized an assembly to raise awareness about women's issues and to dispel the myths surrounding feminism. We also held a car wash to benefit Planned Parenthood and participated in many Pro-Choice rallies and marches. During my four years at Providence College, I have spent much of my free time volunteering for local activist groups, such as the Bristol County Abused Women's Services and the Providence Chapter of the National Organization for Women. Through my work on feminist causes, I have promoted important social issues that are usually ignored by our male-dominated legislatures.

My other social activities have given me invaluable experience in the political and judicial world. By participating in Mock Trial, I have argued difficult cases in front of a real judge. As a result, I have learned much about the legal system and my own personal rights. I also enjoy serving as a delegate for the Model United Nations. By taking a position on a particular political economic or social issue - and debating it with those who assume alternative perspectives – I have learned how the policies that affect the global community are made.

Throughout my work on behalf of feminist causes, I have continued to participate in other social activities to retain a sense of balance in my life. I especially enjoy creative writing, such as plays and poems, and I work as the Features Editor on the campus newspaper. I also play on my women's lacrosse team. My various activities have taught me many things about myself and my place in the world. Most importantly, they have taught me that I must work to create the changes in the world that I want to see, such as equality for women in the global marketplace. By becoming an attorney, I can protect the rights and freedoms that I personally hold dear; ideally, I can also set a positive example for younger women to follow.

Our Assessment: This candidate has won several awards for her Mock Trial experience, which revealed her impressive skills as a debater. In this essay, she reveals her passion for feminism – and the spirit of equality that the term suggests. After reading it, the committee knew that she would be a welcome addition to programs that would allow her to continue to cultivate her skills as a speaker, writer, and advocate.

Feminism

As Anna waited in our office, I marveled at how much she looked like me; we were both short, with dark brown hair and a lithe, athletic build. Yet upon closer scrutiny, our similarities were purely physical. The previous night, while I studied for my psych exam, Anna had been beaten by her abusive husband and was forced to flee with her young child. According to police reports, she had been victimized by her spouse for over five years, yet she always drifted back to him. At just 23, with no education or job skills, Anna couldn't envision any hope of a better future.

For many college students, women like Anna are a sad mystery. In a country with unlimited resources, how could a healthy and smart young woman wind up in such a dismal situation? In my work as a volunteer with Women & Children First, I have learned all too well that Anna's situation is far from unique. Across the globe, women who live in poverty are often victims of physical and emotional abuse. In western nations, they fall prey to abusive boyfriends and husbands who control their behavior and destroy their self-esteem. Even more frightening, many girls in Third World nations are sold into the sex trade, in which they must earn a living by selling their bodies. Without emotional and financial assistance, these women are unable to escape the desperation of their dead-end lives.

As a successful college student, I am blessed with the prospect of a bright future, yet I am painfully aware that I could easily have fallen victim to the same violence as Anna. As a young child, I also struggled with the effects of poverty and sexual abuse. Fortunately, with the help of a qualified therapist, I recovered from the trauma and learned how to build a better life. As a survivor, I am determined to use my skills to provide a voice for others who struggle with the same issues.

Looking back, my traumatic childhood was the catalyst that sparked my passion for learning. At an early age, I began to challenge the limits of my abilities. Despite our limited financial resources, my mother encouraged me to envision a world without boundaries, in which the word "can't" does not exist. As a result, I pursued my education with a vengeance and took the most demanding courses possible. With my eye on a legal career, I chose to major in psychology, to better understand why people do the things they do. In 2010, I will complete my degree in Psychology at Syracuse University, where my student research has focused on memory and eyewitness testimony.

Throughout my undergraduate years, I have been a passionate advocate for the rights of women and children. As a volunteer for Women & Children First, I have been a counselor, mentor, teacher and fundraiser for families in need. I also work for Beloved Lioness, which champions the rights of oppressed women in Third World Countries. In 2009, I volunteered as an assistant consultant for Attorney Sarah Wildman, who specializes in immigration law. Our clients were poor refugees who had fled from violence in their native countries. Some had lost their husbands in civil wars, while others had endured physical and sexual exploitation. All were desperate to remain in the United States. With my background in psychology, I counseled our clients and helped our attorneys translate their testimony between English and Arabic. As a woman who shared their ethnic background, I was a comforting face to many of our female clients, who were hesitant to discuss being molested, raped or sold into prostitution. Their heartbreaking stories opened my eyes to the powerful ways that an attorney can change someone's life. My greatest frustration was that we could not help everyone; with limited resources, many injustices were simply beyond our reach.

Despite the overwhelming work load, I was energized by the chance to defend the rights of people who would otherwise lack a voice in the legal system. I cannot imagine a more satisfying career than serving as an advocate for a non-profit organization that protects the rights of under-represented groups. I am particularly eager to challenge international policies that oppress and exploit women and children. As a United States citizen, I am deeply appreciative of the benefits the country has to offer, including a fair and just legal system. Yet, as an advocate, I know that many people do not receive equal justice because of financial and educational limitations. As an attorney, I will represent indigent clients like Anna, who desperately need my help. In my quest to protect innocent victims from unspeakable violence, I will never give up.

<u>Our Assessment</u>: This is a strong statement from a woman who is committed to serving as an advocate for oppressed and abused women. In this eloquent statement, she states her case clearly and passionately; her multicultural background was particularly well perceived in the admissions process.

Feminism

Growing up in the 1970's, I was mesmerized by the huge social shift in the US. For the first time, women went to college in record numbers and assumed professional roles that were previously unavailable to them. The development of reliable birth control and the sexual revolution gave us freedoms that my mother and grandmother never imagined. I was an inquisitive child of the times. With so many available "flavors," I was eager to taste them all.

After completing my BA in Social Work at Vassar College, I accepted a job with Planned Parenthood of Pittsburgh, where we offer a full range of women's health services, including low-cost gynecological exams, pregnancy testing, birth control counseling and programs to prevent and treat sexually transmitted diseases. I also developed a sex education curriculum that promoted contraception, AIDS awareness and sexual abuse prevention. For many years, our services were heralded in the community and our attorney served in strictly an advisory capacity. Things would soon change….. for the worse.

In the late 1990's, as the tide shifted regarding women's rights, we became the target of right-wing attacks. For many years we were the only facility in Beaver County that provided first trimester pregnancy terminations. Unfortunately, the local Republican Party and their overly zealous supporters resented our commitment to performing services that they personally opposed. Soon, religious protestors began to picket the clinic, accost our patients with religious propaganda, and threaten their lives. Many days, they blocked the entrances to our building, which made it difficult for patients to come and go. We frequently received bomb threats and had our windows broken by demonstrators. Despite my fears, I felt compelled to take a stand against this intimidation.

I volunteered for a Democratic congressional campaign, where I briefed the candidate on abortion rights and sexuality issues in health care reform. I used my position at Planned Parenthood to lobby at the state level against parental notification laws for minors who received abortions. I coordinated grassroots lobbying efforts on pending legislation that would make violent acts committed by clinic protestors part of the proposed "hate crime" bill. I also worked as an advocate for the legalization of the abortion pill RU-486.

In 2008, I served as the manager of Senator Harry Jones' reelection campaign, because I supported his liberal policies on women's health care and civil rights. The position provided me with greater professional responsibility than I had at Planned Parenthood, as I designed ad campaigns, conducted fundraisers and managed hundreds of volunteers. After the Senator's re-election, I assumed the presidency of the newly-created Pennsylvania Women's Health Advocacy Group in Harrisburg. With the help of a lobbyist, we coordinate grassroots strategy programs to promote women's health issues on the state level. In my current position, I research legislation, design lobbying strategies and serve as the liaison with affiliated organizations throughout the state regarding pending policies and bills.

I have derived tremendous personal satisfaction from revamping reproductive health policy and health care reform on the state level, yet I yearn to develop the legal expertise that will allow me to make a greater contribution. Law school will provide the technical skills and professional influence to confront right-wing legislation and initiatives; it will also improve my ability to design and advocate original social policies that benefit women's rights. After law school, I hope to continue working for women's advocacy groups such as Planned Parenthood and the ACLU Reproductive Freedom Project. I am committed to ensuring the survival of women's rights for future generations.

Our Assessment: This author has a long and illustrious career as an advocate for various feminist causes in Pennsylvania, which this statement covers in a few short paragraphs. Although the statement is somewhat dry, it conveys the candidate's commitment to the cause and her future intentions in an eloquent way.

Feminism

In my 12-member class at Sproul High School, Jennifer and I were the only two girls. We had been best friends from the moment her family bought the dairy farm adjacent to ours. Nearly every memory I have of my childhood includes Jennifer's blond ponytails and infectious smile, which could literally light up a room. So, it is probably not surprising to know that Jennifer's death at age 16 was the greatest loss of my life. Even more troubling was the cause: a botched, illegal abortion.

Ironically, I thought I knew everything about Jennifer, but she did not tell me that she was pregnant. I certainly knew nothing about her plans to terminate her pregnancy with the help of a "nurse's aide" in Beaver

Falls. At 16, she was not old enough to obtain a legal abortion in Pennsylvania without obtaining parental consent. For whatever reason, Jennifer obviously felt that she could not solicit her parent's support on the matter. In her despair, she made a sad and fatal choice that could never be undone. Six years later, my lingering anger and grief over Jennifer's senseless death continues to propel my life.

As an adult, I have fought tirelessly for feminist causes through legislation, policy, and grass roots organizing. At the University of Pennsylvania, I began my commitment to reproductive health by designing my own major in women's studies. As part of my coursework, I took courses in feminism and wrote about the troubling legal precedent that recognizes fetal rights. During my senior year, I studied the impact the abortion pill RU 486 might have on the National Health Service, researched the evolving debate about the drug in the European press, and presented my findings at a Women's Studies department seminar.

Outside the classroom, I also gained professional experience as a birth control counselor at the university health clinic. In conjunction with Planned Parenthood of Philadelphia, I edited a sexual education curriculum and designed community programs on contraception, AIDS, and sexual abuse prevention. While teaching a class in Harrisburg, I joined the campaign staff of Senator Arlen Specter, who wanted to reach college voters with his message of support for health care, women's rights and gay rights legislation. This volunteer position taught me how to create an effective political message, manage hundreds of volunteers, and work in coalition with other campaigns.

After graduation, I originally planned to take a year off to work at the state capitol before I applied to law school. Yet my memories of Jennifer have caused me to reconsider that decision. Every day, girls across Pennsylvania face an unenviable obstacle when they try to terminate an unwanted pregnancy. If I delay my plans to become an attorney, I will miss my chance to protect and define their rights. While working on Senator Specter's political campaign, I saw the impact that a passionate advocate can have on a worthy cause. I am applying to law school because I would like to acquire the skills and power I will need to make a bigger difference.

Frankly, I think my perspective is needed. Once elected, even well-intentioned politicians have the "need to serve two masters." Their willingness and ability to promote meaningful change is tempered by competing demands and mixed messages from their constituency. My goal is clear, unshakable and single-minded; I will be a tireless advocate for women's rights. To me, it is not a "cause" or "agenda;" it is making sure, one woman at a time, that reproductive rights are protected. Girls like Jennifer are counting on me.

<u>Our Assessment</u>: This essay is powerful because the author channeled her grief into a meaningful passion that literally transformed her life. After reading it, the committee was excited to think of what she would accomplish with a law degree.

Feminism

"That's not fair." As the only girl in our large family, I was always aware of the many ways in which I was denied equal treatment. At first, I focused my wrath on the trivial injustices at home, such as being "too young" to play softball with my brothers. By late childhood, however, I also became a voice for several injustices outside the walls of my home.

Why, for example, was I not allowed to be an altar boy at church? Why could I not enroll in shop class with my brother Jimmy? Or learn how to wrestle? Although the appeal of these activities might have been fleeting, that really wasn't the point. I hated being told that I couldn't do something because I was the "wrong" sex.

My goal as a student has been to lead the fight against sexual discrimination; likewise, this goal will also guide my future. For the past two summers, I have worked in the Los Angeles law firm of Gloria Allred, who has devoted her life to obtaining justice for women. On the XXXX case, I performed legal research and directly assisted Ms. Allred with trial preparation. Under her guidance, I have learned the inner workings of litigation and I have seen the unfairness that pervades every type of law. My exposure to the opportunities and limitations of the court system has enabled me to evaluate the field with a sense of realism that I would not otherwise possess. Nevertheless, I am commitment to this profession.

Last summer, I participated in UCLA's Public Policy Promotion Program (PPPP), which allowed me to take classes at the UCLA law school. My class in public policy showed me the public interest side of law, which holds the greatest promise for addressing the women's issues that are so important to me. Ideally, this specialty will also allow me to protect the rights of female clients who cannot afford legal assistance.

My classes at UCLA, as well as my participation in the volunteer program at the City of Angels Women's Resource Center, have afforded me the chance to research violence against women, which has become a meaningful interest to me. In a class called "Self-Defense is more than Karate," the center instructs high school students on relationships, HIV/AIDS, dating violence, and sexual assault. After I observed the program, I became certified to teach it, which allows me to disseminate useful advice to women of all ages.

Although fighting unfairness is certainly a driving force, I am also attracted to the law for its ability to change people's values, thoughts and actions. As a writer, I am fascinated by the many similarities between these disciplines. Just as literature tells a story, so does each legal case, be it criminal or civil; the way in which the law applies to each case must be analyzed and constructed. Likewise, both law and literature are instruments of change. Furthermore, they each give a voice to people who traditionally have been silenced. Even if I am a lone voice for fairness, I will make myself heard.

<u>Our Assessment:</u> This essay, although not perfect, is simple, focused and sincere. To enhance the candidate's application, her former boss, Gloria Allred, wrote a glowing recommendation letter on her behalf, which documented her passion for public interest law. As a result, the committee knew that she was a highly motivated and articulate young woman with much to offer the profession.

Feminist

My favorite bedtime stories came from my grandmother Ella, who dazzled me with tales of castles, white knights and beautiful blond princesses. As a young girl, I couldn't imagine anything more wonderful than living the glamorous life I was certain that Ella had lived. How else could she possibly have known so much about love, romance and European royalty?

It was not until my junior year of high school that I learned that Ella had fled from Germany in 1935 to escape the Holocaust. For many years, she and her parents had scrambled around Europe, where they sought shelter and refuge wherever they could find it. After hearing about the atrocities that Ella endured, I was amazed by her ability to not only make peace with anti-Semitism, but to forgive her tormentors. My grandmother, more than anyone else, taught me to be proud of being a American Jew. Nevertheless, her stories about Neo-Nazi demonstrations in front of her synagogue filled me with fear and anger. Learning about this misplaced hatred caused me to examine the legal rights that will prevent Ella's past from becoming my own.

As a journalist, my focus is the freedom of the press and its resulting ability to shape social discourse. While researching my senior thesis, I noticed disturbing trends in my employer's coverage of David Duke's senatorial campaign. Although our publisher knew of his racist and anti-Semitic comments, they failed to report them for nearly a year. When pressed, the publisher claimed that they were "not newsworthy." As a staunch opponent of censorship, I yearned for the newspaper to publish meaningful guidelines regarding what is (and is not) printed.

As a stringer for the Associated Press, I see similar conflicts of interest in what the major papers choose to cover. Amazingly, even the best editors will accept a story on nude sunbathing but will reject one on Louis Farrakhan. Although they realize that Farrakhan has caused a huge controversy, they discount him as a meaningless publicity hound. All I am told is "don't cover it." Likewise, many subsidiaries of *USA Today* have declined to publish the speeches of Catharine MacKinnon and Abba Eban, but have run full-page stories on Lindsay Lohan's love life. According to the media, publicity-hounds in show business, regardless of how vacuous they may be, are of greater importance to the American public than those in religion and politics.

I first discovered the sexist nature of the legal system while writing my senior thesis on the societal influences of the media on our judicial system. My resulting manuscript, which was published by the *Feminist Papers*, concluded that women should not turn to the legal system for protection from the sadistic sexism of hard-core pornography. It seems that man's "right" to view images of obscene violence against women trump those of the underage children who were forced to participate in those acts. The landmark decision in support of pornographers was a defining moment of my life. The more that I examined alternative means of dispute resolution, the more I began to question whether our current system truly provided justice.

My summer internship with the New York City prosecutor's office taught me that the system is easy to manipulate. I answered motion after motion by defense attorneys who knew that if they delayed long enough, the case would be dropped. Likewise, I prepared cases knowing that Judge A would likely impose a far more stringent sentence than Judge B. Although I am not a legal historian, I am certain that the current system bears little resemblance to what our forefathers intended. My motivation for becoming an attorney is to try to fix it.

My grandmother Ella loves the United States because of the equality and freedoms that it affords its citizens, which are defined and protected by our legal system. Certainly, even on our worst days, we provide a modicum of hope that does not exist in other nations. Yet we can certainly do better, both in the development of laws and in their execution. The first step is identifying and eliminating the legal system's current sexual and racist biases. The second step is to raise public awareness of these issues to ensure support. My professional goal is to practice public interest law and to continue as a writer of social commentary. By doing so, I can protect and strengthen the freedoms that my grandmother holds dear.

Our Assessment: This author is a seasoned journalist who has published her work in several prestigious publications. Her eloquent statement, which explains her passion for legal and social justice, gave depth to her application, which was already quite impressive. It showed the reader a side of her that they would never have seen any other way.

Chapter 4: Inspired by a Unique Life Experience

Many candidates use their statements to discuss an experience that had a particular impact on them – or that motivated their application to law school. If you decide to take this approach, you should pick a defining experience that helped you to demonstrate or clarify your values. Ironically, the experience does not necessarily have to be a positive one; many times, we learn the greatest lessons from the challenges and obstacles we face.

A common sense caveat, however: if you choose to discuss a difficult experience, be sure to explain how you have learned and grown from it as a person. Your goal is not to elicit sympathy, but to position yourself as a survivor who has much to offer the law school that accepts you.

Here are several successful personal statements from candidates who were admitted to highly competitive law schools. By design, we have grouped the statements in the following sub-categories:

Inspired by an Illness or Traumatic Experience
Inspired by Religion
Immigration & Travel

To protect the privacy of the writer, the names of all people, classes, schools, places, teams, activities, and companies have been changed.

Inspired by an Illness or Traumatic Experience

There's always a long line of people waiting on the corner of Fifth Street and Washington Boulevard in downtown Boston. Although they look like tourists, they are actually donors who provide the "gift of life" to the District 32 Blood Bank. I have volunteered there since I was 18 years old, when a violent car accident changed my life. Unfortunately, while driving home from school, the bang that I heard wasn't just in my mind, but the sound of a motorcycle hitting my car at 35 mph. Its driver, a kid named Wyatt, was thrown onto a lawn more than 25 feet away. He was badly injured, but was fortunately wearing a helmet. I waited with him until the ambulance came, which was the longest 23 minutes of my life.

Thankfully, my injuries were minor because my car absorbed the bulk of the impact. But Wyatt was another story. His legs and arms were scraped beyond belief; he also had a terrible gash on his right leg that was bleeding profusely. Although Wyatt's injuries were not life-threatening, he needed multiple surgeries to stop his internal bleeding. The hospital faced an immediate dilemma because Wyatt's blood type, A positive, was in short supply. They were desperate for donors.

Although I wasn't a match, my father immediately stepped forward to donate, along with several hospital employees. Accidents like ours were a painful reminder of the urgent need for donors. Within an hour, two reporters from local news stations came to film a segment requesting blood donations. Although I declined to be interviewed about the accident, I was impressed by the hospital's quick call to action and the public's overwhelming response to help an injured boy.

The long-term effects of the accident were overwhelmingly positive. Wyatt recovered from his injuries, survived three months of rehabilitation, and gave up his motorcycle. He is currently in college in California, where he is studying to be a physical therapist. I began my volunteer work at the Blood Bank just six months after the accident and haven't missed a weekend shift in the past four years. I do every task that doesn't require a medical degree, including interviewing donors, taking medical histories, cataloging and transporting blood, and maintaining our computer records. I particularly enjoy interacting with the donors, who are kind and giving people who want to help their fellow humans. I have been touched by donors who faced their fears of needles, AIDS, passing out and developing anemia in order to help a total stranger. I also enjoy my role of teacher, which requires me to debunk rumors about donating blood and putting people's minds at ease.

My volunteer work has inspired me to choose a legal career; I am committed to giving back to the community that has always supported me. Throughout my four years at Harvard, I have spent many hours soliciting donations and volunteers for the Blood Bank. When people question the need, I tell them Wyatt's story and how his life was changed by a few units of blood. It's a shameless ploy, but it usually works. People want to help; they often just need a little nudge to do the right thing. After law school, I plan to give our community a big nudge by dedicating my life to public service. I am sure that Wyatt would be proud.

Our Assessment: This candidate took a risk by discussing a volunteer activity that did not relate directly to the law. Nevertheless, this statement was effective because it explained his commitment to the Blood Bank, which sparked his decision to pursue a career in public service. Combined with his recommendation letters, which documented his tireless work for the Blood Bank, the candidate presented a highly impressive application.

Inspired by an Illness or Traumatic Experience

For residential counselors at the Kenosha Adolescent Drug and Treatment Center, going to work often means going to war. My clients are troubled adolescents who lack basic coping skills in typical life situations. At times, I need to raise my voice and step between clients in order to prevent a fight. Without warning, I have been personally attacked and subjected to cruel and humiliating profanity. Yet, as a soldier in the war against addiction, my ammunition includes empathy, group sessions and non-violent crisis intervention skills. I must do whatever is necessary to reach and help a vulnerable and troubled group of clients.

Yet my job is not what is extraordinary about me; my greatest source of pride is the leadership experience that I acquired at a relatively young age. Prior to college, I was painfully shy in social situations, including the classroom. While other children were told to *stop* talking, I brought home report cards that advised exactly the opposite. How things have changed!

In the rigorous academic environment at the University of Wisconsin, I began my metamorphosis. Success came slowly, and my first English class was a disaster. Looking back at my first failing paper, I am embarrassed to even read it. The following semester, I took a bold risk – several discussion-based classes, in which my peers challenged and changed my modes of thought. Soon, I began to thrive under the pressure of a rigorous curriculum. By seeking extra assistance from the faculty, I got an A in my first English class and excelled in my subsequent courses in interpretive writing.

Through internships and volunteer work, I discovered my tendency to lead by example rather than charisma. I eagerly take on challenges that others are reluctant to assume, including patients with HIV/AIDs, drug and/or alcohol addictions, criminal pasts or a history of perpetrating and/or suffering physical and/or sexual abuse. By working with clients from diverse backgrounds, I have learned to set aside my fears and focus on my client's needs. One weekend, I led a group of volunteer projects in a home for mentally disabled adults. Until we arrived at the placement, I didn't realize that our duties would include helping the adult male residents bathe, brush their teeth, and change their diapers. Leaving my emotion and anxiety aside, I assumed a leadership role and initiated a bathing schedule. By the end of the weekend, I had forgotten my original embarrassment.

During the past few years, I have become a confident leader who is driven to succeed. As I continue to mature, I am eager to expand my existing "comfort level" to include new knowledge and experiences. Clients often tell me about horrific circumstances that I am powerless to change, such as complex legal issues that are beyond my skills as a social worker. As an attorney, I will be able to offer them professional guidance and practical solutions; I also hope to influence the laws and policies that affect the services we provide for the mentally ill. The rigorous legal education I receive at the University of Michigan will allow me to make a meaningful contribution to the city, county, state and federal agencies that must handle these problems with efficiency and compassion.

The diverse student body at the University of Michigan will enhance my ability to represent a heterogeneous group of clients skillfully and ethically. With timely assistance, many clients manage to turn their lives around and become valuable contributors to society. As an advocate, I will use my voice to speak for them and to improve the quality of their lives. After such a long journey to find and understand my own voice, I am determined not to waste it.

Our Assessment: In this essay, the candidate does an artful job of explaining her teenage shyness, which caused her considerable pain during her first year of college. By taking us on her journey to find her own voice, she gets us to root for her and appreciate her accomplishments even more. On a technical basis, the essay also provides an honest and hopeful account of her background and goals, which were an excellent match for the programs she chose.

Inspired by an Illness

Before the threat of a terminal illness, my life was amazingly blessed; I had a great family, a zest for life and every hope for a rewarding future. A sensitive child, my interest in a legal career became clear to me at an early age; I wanted to defend people who could not defend themselves. Long before I understood the technical aspects of the legal field, I knew that I wanted to be an advocate for those who were bullied by others and needed a strong voice in order to fight back.

Throughout high school and college, I worked every summer for an immigration attorney who championed the rights of clients who were trying to gain US citizenship. I felt a deep sense of satisfaction from helping others defend their rights. A recent case was particularly moving to me; we represented a non-citizen who had been a victim of domestic violence. I was honored to do my part to help the woman build a better future.

My undergraduate degree in Political Science was a perfect amalgamation of my passion for cultural and international issues. Just before my senior year at Stanford, however, my hopes for the future vanished in a regrettable moment. During my volunteer work with AIDS patients, I discovered that I had foolishly exposed myself to the possibility of contracting HIV. Within a period of days, my well-planned life turned into a nightmare of fear and recriminations. How could I possibly have let this happen? I should have known better! As I prepared for the LSAT, I was plagued by insomnia. I tried desperately to focus my energy on my schoolwork, yet I was haunted by worries. For several months, no doctor or test could convince me that my life would ever be the same.

As I began my senior year, I decided to postpone my applications to law school and focus on my class work. By immersing myself in school, my suspicions and anxieties eventually waned. From an outsider's perspective, I finished my academic career stronger than ever. In addition to making the dean's list, I worked two part-time jobs, tutored an 11-year old boy after school, completed an independent study with my political science professor and joined several university organizations, including Phi Alpha Delta, the pre-law academic fraternity. Although my fears persisted, I was determined not to let them ruin my life.

By the time I completed my Bachelor's degree in International Economics, I was ready to embrace the future. To celebrate my graduation, I moved to New York and accepted a challenging position at a financial services firm. Although I enjoyed the work, I was continually drawn to a legal career, which would allow me to make a direct impact on the lives of others. During my long year of fearful introspection, I discovered the beauty in every single day. I was determined not to waste another minute of my life.

Thankfully, I have put my fear and shame into the proper perspective. What happened to me was terrible, but it does not negate the character, motivation and skills that I have carefully crafted over the past 23 years. Since high school, I have dedicated my life to building a satisfying career in international law. I cannot imagine a more rewarding future than using my skills to help those who lack the many blessings that I have been given. Hopefully, by pursuing this path I can provide a source of comfort and support when my clients need it the most. I can give them the greatest gift of all – a second chance at a satisfying future.

Our Assessment: Many times, candidates ask us if they should write their statement on a controversial topic, such as HIV. This is a rare case in which the topic worked because of the deft and persuasive way that the author handled it. She did not base the entire statement on the illness; instead, she included it as a secondary topic, after revealing her longstanding interest in the law. By doing so, the candidate gave the reader a full perspective of her talents and skills, which differentiated her from other applicants to top tier programs.

Inspired by Familial Illness

My father was diagnosed with terminal cancer the summer that I turned eight years old. At first, I didn't know how serious it was, only that our summer trip was cancelled when my dad was hospitalized for "tests." Although everyone in the family played down its importance, I could tell by my mother's worried expression that it was serious. I didn't fully comprehend the term "malignant melanoma," but I soon learned that it was a death sentence. My family's life was never the same.

Dad survived for two years after his malignant mole was removed, and for much of that time, I didn't know that his condition was terminal. His oncologist, Dr. Wu, was an optimistic man who encouraged my dad to try every experimental treatment. During the late 80's, this meant a powerful combination of drugs that were administered weekly. My mother and I accompanied dad for chemotherapy at Cedars Hospital every Monday. I still remember the pained expression on his face the moment the IV was inserted. Although Dad tried to be brave for my sake, I could tell that he was nauseated beyond relief. Since mom's religion precluded her from accepting his dismal prognosis, I was totally unprepared for his death. It seemed so cruel, yet strangely comforting, to have a loving, supportive doctor who specialized in death.

Our story would be typical of most cancer patients were it not for our concurrent legal struggles. Dad's insurance company didn't approve of Dr. Wu's proposed treatment plan and refused to pay for it. When my parents challenged their decision, the insurance company mobilized their army of lawyers to fight our claim. They sent long explanations of why our claims were denied, citing "experimental treatments" and "clinician with a misguided international perspective." The bottom line was that they wouldn't pay; they refused to save my father's life. Even at age eight, I knew that this was wrong.

I will always be indebted to Dr. Wu and Cedars Hospital for extending every possible courtesy to my family. Dr. Wu waived his fee for most of the treatments and wrote many detailed letters to the insurance company on our behalf, to document the drug's success and justify its use in my father's case. He didn't give up, even when the drug began to fail and my father was dying. In many ways, this introduction to "managed care" infuriated Dr. Wu as much as it did us. It was a tragic foreshadowing of the future of medicine.

My mother faced bills for my father's treatment that she could never pay in the course of her lifetime. Rather than declare bankruptcy, she continued the fight with the insurance company after my father's death. She hired an attorney, William Wise, to represent us in our battle. Her motivation was two-fold: after years of faithfully paying her insurance premiums, she felt that the company was liable. She was also angry that they kicked us when we were down. William Wise accepted the case on a contingency basis, although that was a rarity in the 1980's. Fortunately for us, he had the patience of a saint and the skills of a master. After seven long years of litigation, we settled out of court for enough money to pay my father's outstanding medical bills. More importantly, the insurance company finally approved Dr. Wu's treatment for melanoma, which ensures that other policy holders can avoid the same uphill battle for compensation.

I'm not sure what was the determining factor for me to enter the legal profession: the fine example of William Wise or my anger at the insurance company. Each year, millions of Americans are diagnosed with terminal illnesses that do not respond to the FDA-approved treatments that insurance companies will cover. Although many experimental and alternative drugs are effective, they are prohibited in the US without FDA approval. In the long years of mandatory "testing," millions die because they cannot afford to pay for the drugs without insurance coverage. This vicious cycle is misguided and wrong.

By becoming an attorney, I can lobby for increased funding for the FDA testing and approval of drugs. I will also form a watchdog group to monitor the performance of insurance companies and how they treat their clients. Ideally, as time permits, I will do pro bono work, like William Wise, to represent patients who lack the resources to pay for experimental drugs out of their own pockets. No one should die because of governmental bureaucracy.

My summer internships in William Wise's law firm have provided me with hands-on experience as a legal aid. I would like to think that both of my parents, now deceased, would be proud of the path I am taking. Both died under the terrible stress of needless litigation. They were forced to fight red tape when they should have been concentrating on their health. I am committed to fighting for others in that position, to make their final days as stress-free as possible.

Our Assessment: This candidate struggled with this essay because he could not think of a "clever" way to open it. Ultimately, he took the advice of his advisor to simply write from the heart. The resulting draft, although long, is honest, detailed, and memorable. No one else could tell this story, which explains the compelling reason that the candidate wanted to become an attorney. His passion to reform insurance laws made a powerful impression on the committee.

Inspired by a Familial Illness

Ambulance ride: $75.00
Emergency hospital visit: $825.00
Cat scan: $2,000.00
Medication: $7,000.00
Surgery: $65,000.00

Extended hospital stay: $15,000.00

LIFE: PRICELESS

Although money can buy many things, life itself is priceless. Two years ago, my family confirmed that sentiment during an unexpected medical emergency. The gorgeous day started like many others, with the sun beaming, the birds chirping, and children laughing as they started their summer vacations. I was eager to change into my bathing suit and go to the beach with my brother Joaquin.

Despite the summer heat, I felt an arctic chill when I entered my parents' house. The ominous tone in my mother's voice conveyed the gravity of her news. Joaquin had been diagnosed with a rare brain disorder called chira malformation, which meant that his brain was too big for his skull. As a result, it caused cerebral bleeding down his spine and a loss of sensation throughout his body. In absolute shock, I could not comprehend the news. My mother continued to talk, although I desperately wanted her to stop. Maybe if she didn't say it again, it wouldn't be true. Yet my father's tears confirmed my worst suspicions. The situation was grave.

Sadly, the news got even worse. When my brother turned 18 a month earlier, his health insurance lapsed and he was no longer covered under the family policy. Sadly, my parents couldn't possibly afford the $100,000 cost of Joaquin's surgery. With no other treatment options, they began to panic. How in the world could they save their son? Initially, they blamed each other for the predicament. My mother couldn't imagine why my father had allowed Joaquin's health plan to lapse, while my father couldn't imagine that anything this devastating could happen. For more than a week, the house seemed like a morgue.

At the hospital, Dr. Fernandez suggested that my parents read the "fine print" in their insurance policy to determine if the firm was still liable for my brother's health. As a researcher for attorney Carlos Vasquez-Nunes, I immediately put my investigative skills to work on my brother's behalf. I searched every line for a detail that might relate to Joaquin's case. Finally, during my third reading of the policy, I found the miraculous loophole. Right there, in the fine print that our doctor stressed, I read: "ANY POLICY HOLDER BETWEEN THE AGES OF 18 TO 21 NO LONGER ATTENDING SCHOOL WILL BE COVERED WITH THE FULL BENEFITS THAT THEIR POLICY OFFERS FOR A GRACE PERIOD OF NINETY DAYS."

I re-read the critical clause several times, silently counting the number of days that had elapsed since my brother's birthday. I even rubbed my eyes several times to make sure I wasn't dreaming. After all this time, there it was, right in front of my eyes: my brother's salvation. When I got home that day, Joaquin knew at first glance that I had found the miracle, as the glow from my smile reflected back into his eyes. "Carlina, you did it!" As we embraced our parents, we shared tears of joy, acknowledging that a single phrase in the contract literally meant the difference between life and death.

My brother's surgery was the most successful operation ever performed on such a case, which set the standard for future chira malformation surgeries. He is currently pursuing his dream of attending the New York School of Design in Manhattan. Law school is the culmination of my dreams, which will provide the formal training I will need to make a difference in the lives of others. At the time of Joaquin's illness, I had already worked in a law office for several years and was committed to attending law school. Yet my family's experience with the insurance policy provided a tremendous personal incentive to continue my work. Using the skills from my job, I helped to save the most important person in my life. Others aren't always so fortunate.

On a daily basis, people enter into agreements that can have negative legal ramifications. Sadly, many sign away their rights without understanding the risks. As my family learned, the language of a specific clause may ultimately determine a loved one's survival. By becoming an attorney, I will help clients understand the contracts they sign and their inherent implications. Hopefully, I will help other families find the same miracle that we were privileged to enjoy.

Our Assessment: This essay, although long, is heartfelt and memorable. The author's love for her brother – and her satisfaction in helping to save his life, gave the reader a glimpse into her generosity of character. In their recommendation letters, her employers confirmed that she was an excellent fit for a program in public interest law.

Inspired By Mother's Illness

Three years ago, a malignant brain tumor destroyed my mother's pituitary gland. As recently as 1990, her cancer would have been a death sentence, but, thanks to the amazing breakthroughs in medical research, my mother is still here with us. Twice a day, she takes a genetically engineered growth hormone to replace the secretions that her body can no longer produce naturally. This miraculous technology has given back to her a portion of what she lost to the tumor.

One of the biggest innovations in medicine has been the use of bacteria to genetically engineer drugs such as insulin and growth hormone. For patients like my mother, they have literally made the difference between life and death. Current research suggests that growth hormone might also be an effective treatment for ailments as diverse as osteoporosis, severe burns and infertility. As a witness to its benefits, I am a staunch supporter of its research and development. Yet, to no one's surprise, there is a dark side to its availability and use.

Although many people could benefit from growth hormone, it can also be abused for athletic purposes. Football great Lyle Alzado appeared on national television to ask the public to refrain from misusing growth hormones, which he believed were responsible for his brain cancer. Before his death, he urged Congress to limit the availability of the drug to ensure that it does more good than harm. Mr. Alzado also asked the government to stop funding any type of related genetic research.

I respectfully disagree with his position. This research has allowed scientists to locate genes that are linked to diseases such as cystic fibrosis, sickle cell anemia and Huntington's disease. Eventually, this knowledge could yield better treatments or even a cure for these disorders. I cannot imagine anyone finding fault with important discoveries that can potentially save lives; to me, their benefits to society far outweigh the potential for abuse.

Throughout the 20th century, nearly every aspect of modern medicine has reaped the rewards of technological advancements, which are growing at an exponential rate. Every door we open leads to more doors, which may contain secrets as well as revelations. Granted, with every gain comes the possibility of abuse, yet does this justify ending an entire research program? The majority of the population can only imagine the excitement of opening one of these doors for the first time. They know in their hearts that it could be *their* loved one who benefits from the resulting technology. In my mind, the answer is not stopping this research, but properly regulating it to ensure its optimal implementation. The potential benefits to people like my mother are too significant to dismiss.

Throughout this journey, I learned more about the disease process, the legal implications of new technologies, and my own desire to guide the discussions that regulate their use. Fortunately, my family's battle had a happy ending; my mother went into remission and my darkest fears did not materialize. Nevertheless, her strength and courage remain a constant source of inspiration to me. By watching her cheat death and retain her faith in God, I have come to share her confidence that we will greet the future with a shared sense of hope and optimism. My fondest wish is that other families enjoy the amazing breakthroughs that God has provided for us. With progressive and compassionate laws regarding experimental drug protocols, they can.

<u>Our Assessment</u>: This statement eloquently and persuasively presents the candidate's position on the off-label use of growth hormones, which saved her mother's life. It also revealed her motivation to enroll in law school and pursue a career in pharmaceutical regulation.

Inspired by Religion

Like many students, I was terribly shaken by the terrorist attacks of 9/11, which came at a time when I felt particularly lost and vulnerable. Several of my friends sought refuge in drugs and alcohol, which provided a temporary respite from their grief and pain. Others became consumed with thoughts of revenge, either through a direct attack on Osama bin Laden, or through the eventual war in Iraq. I, on the other hand, simply felt paralyzed by the senseless destruction of everything that I held dear. I couldn't imagine how I could possibly survive with the terrible pain in my heart.

In my darkest moment, I knelt on the floor of my room and considered the question of my faith. In my first twenty years of life, I had not given much thought to my religion or what I believed. However, a long talk with my pastor had produced questions within me that needed meaningful answers. All at once, I knew that I wanted to live a life that would honor God. The clarity of that moment made me weep. Rising from my knees and wiping the tears off my face, I realized that I had changed in only a few moments. My decision to become a Christian was a momentous turning point in my life, which had a permanent impact on my outlook.

Embracing God and the Christian faith ignited an intellectual fire in me that brought with it an unquenchable thirst for knowledge. I voraciously read every theology book I could find; I was particularly inspired by Saint Augustine, who saw "all truth as God's truth." With this in mind, I decided to become a teacher who would guide and nurture young minds from a Christian world view. By expanding my perspective of world issues, I would be better prepared to engage the minds of my future students and answer tough questions about the actions of those who defy Gods' laws.

Emotionally, my discovery of God has given me a more compassionate attitude towards others. The Bible teaches us that all individuals are created in the image of God and are thereby worthy of dignity and respect. From this lesson, I developed a feeling of responsibility for those who suffer and need help from others. To lessen their pain, I began to visit senior citizens at one of the retirement communities in my city. Each Saturday, I spend time talking to them and helping them perform their daily functions. I have also started to volunteer at my church, where I serve as an assistant to the pastor. As a leader, I feel a deep sense of satisfaction in helping the children develop good moral character.

Ever since that first moment of understanding, my faith in God has served as my driving force to reach my goals. It has armed me with a clear vision of who I want to be and what I want to do with my life. Because of this inner determination, I have decided to pursue a legal career, which will allow me to serve as an advocate for others; I am particularly eager to promote faith-based, social service initiatives that provide people with compassionate answers to life's most difficult questions. In the aftermath of 9/11, my beliefs taught me to view every challenge as an opportunity to grow as an individual and to inspire my family and friends with the strengths that my faith gives me. How we live reveals our deepest convictions about the world. In the past decade, I have offered my life as proof of my convictions. As for the terrorists, I am leaving their fate in God's hands, who will eventually deliver the ultimate judgment.

<u>Our Assessment</u>: We are often asked if candidates should write essays about their religious and spiritual beliefs. Depending on the author's intention, it may (or may not) be risky. Our best advice is to remember the goal of the statement, which is to reveal your best self to the reader. If your essay is positive in nature, helps to explain your character, and promotes a spirit of love and inclusion, then it will not offend anyone. But if the essay is opinionated or divisive, it may not be worth the risk.

This essay works because it is sincere, concise, and informative. It helps the reader understand who the author is and what she will bring to the school that accepts her. The statement was particularly well-received at Catholic law schools, which shared the candidate's commitment to faith-based programs and services.

Inspired By Religion

According to popular opinion, being Christian and being a free thinker are mutually exclusive. I have spent my entire lifetime debunking this perception. In high school, our principal called an assembly to explain the fire at Waco that killed David Koresh and his followers. In our small Dallas suburb, the actions of the FBI left many people frightened and uncertain. Clearly, violence was no solution to a religious stalemate. Nevertheless, I recoiled at the police officer's assertion that the FBI's actions were justified. I raised my hand and asked in a feeble voice, "We weren't there. How can we possibly know what happened?" No one offered a response.

The high school assembly was the first time that I demonstrated my willingness to think for myself, but it was certainly not the last. I was encouraged to be a critical thinker in my Bible classes as well. Because religion is a living, breathing entity, it survives by being discussed and shared by its followers. People often claim that to question the Bible is to reveal its flaws. I disagree. In difficult times, sharing relevant passages from the Bible with trusted loved ones has comforted me and revealed alternative meanings. It has made me a stronger, more focused man. Consequently, I have always sought the same level of interaction in my classroom discussions, in order to obtain a better education.

Unfortunately, not every teacher welcomed such dialogue. In my American Literature class, I questioned Henry David Thoreau's perception that materialism was inherently corrupt. My teacher, Mr. Kringle, dismissed my query, claiming that I wasn't qualified to criticize the author. I was disturbed by his insistence that I accept Thoreau's view at face value. More importantly, I remained convinced of my position because no one could satisfactorily refute my arguments.

Even in my advanced classes, my questions are often ignored. In my junior course in Government, a visiting professor criticized libertarianism in a manner that was blatantly unfair. Sadly, I was the only student who was willing to defend the concept of theistic evolution. My willingness to speak my mind was enhanced by my semester in Switzerland, when I attended a school that was populated by agnostics and atheists. Although my classmates and I held diametrically opposing views on faith, we engaged in stimulating discussions that forced us to examine and articulate our views. I emerged from the semester with a broader perspective not just of the Swiss culture and language, but of the intelligence and grace of its people. By defending their perspectives without discounting mine, my classmates demonstrated a level of maturity that I hope to attain in law school.

As a result of my religion, I feel happier and more peaceful than I ever dreamed possible. In a world in which few people are flexible or passionate enough to engage in intelligent discourse, I will always seek out the kindred souls who are willing to be my teachers. My goal, as always, is to develop my mind by exposing myself to the broadest possible sources of thoughts and opinions. What better way to confirm my own?

Our Assessment: This statement is risky because it does not discuss the candidate's motivation and goals. However, it does an excellent job of revealing his strengths as a thinker and his ability to view alternative viewpoints with intelligence and respect. Combined with his recommendation letters, which discussed his internships at a law firm and the district attorney's office, the candidate's application was quite compelling.

Inspired by International Travel - Peace Corps

After graduating from Notre Dame University, I served for two years as a Peace Corps volunteer in Belize. During this time, I worked on several development projects, including the construction of an elementary school in an area that had been ravaged by Hurricane Hugo. My experience left me with mixed feelings about what is realistically achievable in poor and developing countries. In our case, trying to build a school in an area that lacked safe water and reliable health care seemed like a critical misuse of resources. I questioned whether the United States had misjudged the priorities in Belize or had been given erroneous information. The net result was that I seldom felt that I was making a lasting difference in the children's lives. Without good health, they were not able to learn. As Maslov noted in his hierarchy, until survival is certain, people are unable to focus on their higher needs.

Ironically, I found the greatest potential for change in the area of manufacturing, which has enjoyed tremendous growth in the past several years. To reduce costs, American apparel firms have outsourced their work to textile factories in nations such as Belize. Contrary to what I learned in my business classes, these plants were not abusive or exploitive; the workers were efficient, healthy, and grateful for a reliable job that allowed them to support their families. In fact, the female workers that I met in Belize earned more money in the factories than they would earn in the fields, and they enjoyed the added benefits of a sedentary job. For the first time, they could support themselves without relying on the generosity of their husbands and parents. They felt empowered, not exploited.

As expected, these so-called "sweat shops" had a ripple effect on other aspects of the economy. When manufacturing wages became higher than that of domestic workers, the hotels and restaurants had to pay more money to retain their staff. Likewise, when factories began to offer reduced-price day care to their employees, they attracted so many applications that other businesses were forced to offer comparable benefits to retain their own workers. Despite the media's focus on exploitative and abusive situations in the factories, I saw a population of hardworking people who were eager to embrace the opportunities that outside employment brings. I also recognized that "outsourcing" was not a dirty word; in fact, it is a viable solution for companies that want to offer quality products at a low cost by building factories in poor and developing nations.

As American businesses increase their trade on a global basis, there will be an ongoing need for qualified people to develop and enforce labor codes that benefit the corporations and their workers. A law degree will give me the credentials I will need to draft relevant policies for US investments in Latin America. Ideally, it will also allow me to create the infrastructure that is required to stimulate the sort of healthy growth that these nations need to become viable players in the global economy.

Our Assessment: Many candidates write about their Peace Corps experiences, but few have the confidence to write an essay this strong and focused. By sharing her insight into the manufacturing opportunities in

Belize – and disputing common misconceptions about the safety and working conditions in the factories she visited, this candidate differentiated herself from other applicants who had a comparable background. She also showed her strong fit for programs in international business law.

Inspired by International Travel

One of my parents' favorite stories is about my desperate need for a diaper change on a trip to Singapore. Just two years old, I didn't realize that my furtive cries provided an effective diversion for two border guards who had taken an obsessive interest in our travel itinerary! With their passion for travel, my parents began to visit exotic lands while I was still in diapers. After my birth in Vietnam, we traveled extensively throughout Europe and Africa before moving to Taiwan, where my father worked as an airline pilot. These early international experiences have inspired my deep appreciation for different people and cultures. When I look at my passport, I cherish each country's stamp as a medal of honor, for it represents the rich environment in which I matured from a child to a young adult.

Some trips were carefree adventures. In 1990, we explored Bali, which was the home of one of my father's co-pilots. For several weeks, her family showed us many pristine and secluded beaches, including one where we spent a leisurely day of ocean exploration. Draped over the edge of a drifting Indonesian sea canoe, I watched the colorful fish dart about the rays of sun that pierced the clear blue water. Other trips were more historically significant. In 1993, we traveled to Israel, where my father and I observed several families gathering at the edge of the river to prepare for a sacred ritual. We decided to participate. Holding hands, my father and I descended the earthen-colored stone steps until we reached the edge of the river. We paused before we stepped into the water, which is considered sacred. In the company of the native families, we were humbled to be part of their meaningful congregation.

In retrospect, my less popular destinations provided the most lasting memories and thought-provoking experiences. At age ten, I traveled with my father to China during the first year it opened its border to tourism. While traveling up the Min River, we explored the rural countryside, including several small villages that had never been visited by Caucasians. The authorities cautioned us against entering certain (poor) towns, but their admonition simply made the idea more enticing. As we walked down the narrow dirt roads, all eyes were upon us. I lingered for a moment at a fruit stand, as fifty people crowded around me. The villagers had never seen a foreigner before, much less a little girl with long blond hair and light eyes. At the time, I didn't appreciate the moment's historical significance, simply the desire to establish some kind of connection. As I exchanged glances with the villagers, I offered a faint, nervous smile. Gradually, they returned my congenial expression with comprehension and mutual curiosity. Without words, we built a small, unforgettable bridge between our two inexplicably different cultures.

After graduating from high school in 2005, I enrolled in several classes at Pomona College, where I discovered my passion for education. While building a foundation for my future, I came to appreciate a basic difference between the American and Taiwanese cultures. For many Americans, professional and financial success is a driving force of daily life and a measure of personal validation. In contrast, money plays a less critical role in Asian society, which places equal importance on family, traditions and community involvement. For me, California represented the land of opportunity, where all people (regardless of age, race, religion, or gender) could pluck the fruits of their individual efforts and skills. I was determined to embrace this challenge and discover my innate potential.

Throughout the ensuing years, I came to appreciate the United States for the abundant opportunities it affords its citizens. As a woman who has built her life around the American ideal of achievement, I feel empowered to select and pursue my own dreams. Ultimately, by surviving my initial culture shock, I developed the perseverance to overcome obstacles and to define my own unique role in society. As an ambitious researcher, self-sufficient homeowner and dedicated honor student, I have attained goals that would not have been possible in Taiwan. By entering law school, I hope to begin my transition into a career that provides a balance between my success as a financial analyst and my passion for international relations.

Our Assessment: This essay is risky because it is long, descriptive, and not "on topic" regarding the candidate's credentials for law school. Nevertheless, it shows the reader a side of herself that they would never have known about any other way. By discussing her travel experiences and how they broadened her perspective, the author distinguished herself from other candidates who had similar credentials. Thankfully, the rest of her application (GPA, LSAT scores, and recommendation letters) was extraordinary – and proved that she had the intelligence, character, and analytical skills that are necessary to excel in law school. As a result, the author had the luxury of writing a descriptive essay on a far more personal topic.

Inspired by International Travel

The Body: As I trudged through the sludge-filled Blind River, my stomach churned from the stench of dead and decaying animals. Despite my recent marathon training, I was pushed to my limits by the grueling conditions in rural Louisiana. My passion for adventure inspired me to participate in this project along the contaminated river, which was twenty miles from the nearest city. However, during the intensely challenging conditions in this bug-infested terrain, I concentrated on the goal of my work: to conduct environmental sampling to determine if the toxins from an abandoned factory were responsible for the dramatic increase of rare cancers among the local residents. Despite our difference in age and background, I related to the villagers' concerns regarding the carcinogens. Having lost a loved one to cancer, I empathized with their grief and fear.

The Mind: My father's death from cancer when I was ten taught me a harsh lesson regarding the value of education. Without a college degree, my mother could not find employment that paid more than minimum wage. Starting at age twelve, I helped to support our household by delivering newspapers, washing dishes at a restaurant, and shoveling horse manure at a local farm. I rigorously pursued academic excellence as a way to avoid the hardships my mother had endured. My father's death not only pushed me to succeed academically, but inspired my interest in public health. His cancer was partially attributable to his exposure to Agent Orange, which permeated the Vietnamese village where his Army unit had served. Fifteen years later, only three members of his unit are still alive.

The Community: As an adult, I continue to value the warmth and support in the close-knit town in which I was raised. At the same time, I also enjoy traveling from town to town as a public health investigator. Every community I visit provides a new opportunity to increase public awareness regarding health and environmental issues. Over the years, I have received deep satisfaction from the "human" aspects of my research, rather than the scientific details. By listening to the residents of Louisiana, I learned about the conditions at the abandoned factory and cultivated the friendship and trust of the people in the community. I recently brought my fellow classmates in Philadelphia on a "toxic tour" of several disadvantaged neighborhoods to increase local awareness of environmental health problems. My goal was to show real-life examples of class topics in our own community and to encourage my students to lobby for improvements on a local level.

The Future: Through research, travel and family experiences, I have observed several crises in public health that require immediate intervention. In some cases, like the contamination in Louisiana, legal action will be required to remove the toxic waste and restore healthy living conditions. Other cases simply require the development and implementation of a solid educational program throughout the nation. My passion to solve these problems has reinforced my long-term aspiration to work as an advocate for public health. In my heart, I know that my calling is to infuse the nation with a much-needed sense of balance in making decisions that affect the environment and health. Since early childhood, I have invested my energy in promoting these causes in every aspect of my life. Law school is the next step on my exhilarating educational journey.

Our Assessment: This author used sub-headings to group her topics in a logical way. The breadth of her experiences, which confirmed her interest in environmental law, set her apart from other candidates with similar goals.

Inspired by International Travel

"Help them, please. They have done nothing wrong." The elderly woman wept softly as she told me the story in her native Korean. As I listened in silence, my tape recorder captured the details about the FBI raid at her home the previous evening. The woman's two sons, who did not speak a word of English, had unknowingly signed several credit card applications that contained false information. When the FBI came to investigate, they broke into the woman's house in the middle of the night and took the stunned suspects into custody. Their poor mother, who writhed at the injustice, begged for my help.

As a journalist and reporter for *US Korea*, the largest Korean newspaper in New York, I was no stranger to the unexposed problems within Korean-American communities. Sadly, the obstacles the two men faced were typical of those of most new immigrants, who lack a clear understanding of American laws, policies and culture. Far too often, their ignorance leaves them in precarious situations with little or no recourse. In this case, the accused were eventually sent back to Korea because they failed to understand or adapt to the expectations of the mainstream American culture.

As a first generation Korean-American, I travelled extensively as a child, which taught me many priceless lessons. Starting at age 12, I lived in several places, such as Thailand, Singapore and Taiwan, which were evolving and unpredictable. During this period, I met diverse people from around the world, whose distinct thoughts and ways of life sculpted me into a person of broader perspective and maturity. In every new society I visited, I observed the pain of refugees and the oppression of non-democratic governments. By experiencing these environments first-hand, I learned special lessons that I could never have internalized any other way.

Although jumping into a new environment was exciting to me, each settlement brought its own set of difficulties. In every new place, I was "different" from other teenagers. In Bangkok, I endured stares from strangers because of my unusual appearance and outfits. In Singapore, I struggled to speak a new language at school, which threatened my success as a student. Fortunately, my refusal to be ashamed by my "strangeness" provided me with a strong sense of confidence. By overcoming these cultural barriers, I became a strong communicator who understands other people's perceptions, regardless of their age or background. This insight enables me to negotiate solutions to problems that others cannot resolve. Eventually, I realized that a legal career would enable me to use my unique strengths in a socially meaningful way.

When I first told my parents that I wanted to go to law school, they gently tried to dissuade me. In the Korean community, law school is considered the domain of natural born Americans, rather than immigrants. In my parents' minds, I would experience a tougher course because of my disadvantaged status as a Korean woman. My deeply traditional father even worried that my short height might hinder my progress as a litigator. Despite my family's misgivings, I never doubted that my determination and competence would compensate for any superficial differences I may bring to the profession. In fact, once they realized the power of my conviction, my parents became my strongest supporters.

As a journalist for *US Korea*, I used my voice to bring attention to critical issues in the Korean-American community, yet I usually could not solve the underlying problem or injustice. As an attorney, I will have the skills I will need to protect people's rights and promote change. In all of my endeavors, I have felt the most successful and fulfilled when I have helped someone in need. Contrary to conventional belief, I believe that my status as an Asian immigrant is an advantage, because I have the flexibility to fit into both the mainstream and minority cultures. This is my "American vision," as opposed to the non-specific "American Dream" that most immigrants have. My goal is not a fantasy, but an organized and attainable plan with a clear "vision" for success.

When I ended my interview with the Korean woman whose sons had been unjustly arrested, she squeezed my hand and told me that I should become a lawyer. I was honored that she thought I had the potential to achieve such an ambitious goal. Now, the woman's words are carved in my heart as a reminder of my life's mission; as a lawyer, I will use my education and experience on behalf of those who are less fortunate. I will help them to secure the rights and freedoms to which they are rightfully entitled.

Our Assessment: This statement, although long, reveals the candidate's multicultural background and experience as a reporter. Her unique perspective brought much-needed diversity to her law school class.

Inspired by Personal or Familial Immigration

In difficult times, I am reminded of Friedrich Nietzsche's quotation, "What does not destroy me, makes me stronger." Ironically, when my family moved from Bahrain to the United States in 1999, I did not realize the many challenges I was about to face. On the surface, we were a typical immigrant family that was adjusting to life in a new culture. Blessed with good jobs and a solid marriage, my parents were determined to provide my brother and me with a promising future. Sadly, their love and support were no match for the insidious problem that invaded our home: my older brother's battle with schizophrenia, which began when he was 17 years old.

In hindsight, my brother's illness was not just a family crisis, but a turning point in my childhood. At age 13, when other girls were obsessed with clothes and boys, I was overwhelmed by the many problems that accompanied my brother's diagnosis. In addition to his illness, he also abused illegal drugs, which made his behavior more dangerous and erratic. My brother's problems soon became the sole focus of our family's energy, as my parents invested all of their resources to help him get well. Unfortunately, their efforts became increasingly futile. As my brother continued to refuse treatment, my father became severely depressed and was forced to file for bankruptcy. My mother became a workaholic, which left little time and energy for my needs. On an emotional level, I felt like I was completely alone.

Yet, as Nietzsche predicted, I ultimately became stronger and more focused by surviving this trauma. At a young age, I understood that bad choices could have devastating implications. In our family, my brother's decisions to consume illegal drugs and to refuse psychiatric treatment forced me to assume an adult role in our family far sooner than I was ready to do so. When I was 15, I accompanied my mother to bail my brother out of jail. To our horror, he had been placed in an isolation cell because he had attempted suicide the previous night. Amazingly, I somehow managed to survive a level of dysfunction that no child should be forced to endure.

As I matured, I became obsessed with the concept of personal responsibility. Although I loved my brother, the ramifications of his poor choices were a powerful incentive for me to make better decisions in my own life. With no external prodding, I became a willful young woman who was determined to achieve. Each time we moved, I adapted quickly to my new surroundings and excelled in the classroom. I fought hard to become responsible, respected and reliable. During times of crisis, I was the rational one who could solve problems and provide support for those who were paralyzed by grief and fear. Although I was just a teenager, I was already a survivor.

After my mother and I returned to Bahrain, I began to plan for the future. Despite my lack of funds, I completed a translator course and accepted a job with Trans Global Airlines. Because I was fluent in five languages, I worked on three continents, which gave me a wonderful opportunity to travel and meet new people. During this time, I became appalled by a number of international legal crises, such as the increasing reports of human trafficking across various borders. I began to envision the many ways I could improve society if I pursued a legal career in the United States. Although I hated to leave my family behind, I refused to abandon my goal. In 2007, I moved to New York and began my undergraduate classes at the Fordham University, where I balanced my demanding coursework with a full-time job. With hard work and dedication, I will receive my degree in International Relations in Spring 2011 in preparation for a legal career.

For many survivors of troubled families, their only legacies are grief and shame. Fortunately, I have avoided such a dismal fate. By helping my parents weather an emotional storm, I developed the tools to tackle the inevitable challenges that life presents. I also developed a strong internal compass that guides all aspects of my personal and professional behavior. After coming so far, I am eager to embrace the challenges of law school, where I will bring a vibrant international perspective to class discussions. I will also bring the strength and tenacity of a survivor, who is determined to give back to society by becoming an attorney of integrity and persuasion.

Our Assessment: This essay is risky because it reveals considerable information about the candidate's childhood, which was admittedly difficult. Nevertheless, by explaining how those experiences made her a stronger and more effective person, the author turned the essay into a masterful piece that showcases her personal strengths. Combined with her recommendation letters, which confirmed her effectiveness in stressful situations, the candidate's application was incredibly powerful.

Chapter 5: Experience in a Different Profession

Although most law school candidates are recent college graduates, some are significantly older than their peers, with advanced degrees and several years of work experience. For these candidates, the personal statement is a golden opportunity to update the committee on what you have accomplished since you graduated from college. Ideally, your essay should also explain the type and extent of your professional experiences and how they have influenced your goals.

Additionally, the committee will may wonder why you are seeking a law degree after working for many years in another profession. If you can provide this insight in your personal statement, the admissions committee will be able to confirm your personal and professional fit for a legal career.

Here are several excellent personal statements from older and non-traditional candidates who gained admission to highly competitive law schools. By design, we have grouped them into the following categories:

Scientists & Engineers
Artists, Writers & Musicians
Experience in Social Services
Older Candidates
Career Switch
JD/MBA Applicants

To protect the privacy of the candidate, the names of all people, classes, schools, places, and companies have been changed.

Scientists / Engineers

I have spent my entire life afraid of salad bars - actually, not the bars themselves, but the sulfites that are sprayed on the green leafy vegetables. I am allergic to sulfites, as are over 10 million other Americans, yet they are routinely used to enhance the green color of produce in restaurants and cafeterias. This is actually a great idea, unless you are allergic to them.

My parents gathered a mountain of evidence about sulfites after they learned of my allergy. It seems that they don't pose a "sizable risk" to the public and "offer great tangible benefits" to food distributors everywhere. Sulfites are a food enhancer, which is a chemical agent that gives salad eaters a "warm fuzzy" by making their greens a little greener. As a result, the FDA approved their use without a hitch. My parents often sarcastically ask what kind of jerk would approve something so dangerous. Although we may never know that person's name, I promise you that I will be the attorney who ultimately gets them banned.

Thankfully, thus far, I have avoided a serious sulfite reaction by carrying a portable test kit with me whenever I eat out. In an instant, I can touch a piece of food with an indicator strip and determine if sulfites are present. Although the kit keeps me out of danger, many people can't afford them and others don't even know that they have the allergy. Consequently, at least 25 deaths occur in the US each year as a direct result of allergic reactions to sulfite. To me, the only serious long-term solution is to either ban them or to enforce serious labeling regulations. Unfortunately, the FDA has no interest in either option.

As an undergraduate student, I began to champion my battle against sulfites. My class project for my Analytical Chemistry class was to improve the original test strip that identifies sulfites. The current version is a paper strip that relies on a color indicator. It can easily be misread and disintegrates quickly if stored in a warm, moist environment. Consequently, users in tropical climates must refrigerate them for several months of the year. As expected, these limitations greatly reduce the strip's effectiveness. My prototype uses a heat-stable dye that withstands temperature and humidity extremes to 120 degrees F and 100 % RH, respectively. It also offers a more dramatic color delineation in its dye, which makes the results easier to interpret. I have applied for a patent for this strip and am currently awaiting the decision of the US Patent Office.

Down the road, I believe that the FDA needs more people like me, who will use their science background and legal expertise to promote public safety. For several reasons, I am a good candidate for them. I have a great background in biochemistry, am passionate about food regulation, and am an energetic public speaker. After law school, I hope to leverage these strengths by pursuing a career at the FDA or with an advocacy group that monitors them.

I think that my proposed role is necessary and overdue. Any agency that approves sulfites, breast implants, Phen-Fen and aspartame without adequate testing needs a new influx of talent. They also need to adjust their priorities and focus on issues that directly impact public health. Sadly, the FDA routinely drops the ball on issues that could potentially harm a lot of people, which destroys the public's faith in them. Compared to other agencies, the FDA has an important job; they must regulate and monitor commercial food products to ensure that all Americans can eat safely. With my help, they can do it better.

Our Assessment: This candidates' original draft was a long, boring, technical-laden piece that was difficult to understand. In the revision process, he abandoned that approach and simply wrote from the heart. The resulting draft is extremely informal, but gives the reader keen insight into his personality; it also explains his personal motivation, which the committee would not have known about any other way.

Scientists / Engineers (Part-time JD/MBA program)

"People with vibrant personalities do NOT work in research laboratories." Six years later, my sister's assessment of my introverted personality continues to hurt my pride. Although I would love to dispute her assessment, I know that scientists and engineers are not the best communicators, at least, not with non-scientists. In my mind, this isn't a character defect or even a lack of initiative; it is simply a reflection of the single-minded excitement that we have for our own profession. When we meet a kindred spirit who speaks our own "techno-language," well, everyone else just fades into the background.

As an undergraduate student, my motivation to attend a large school like Yale was to become part of a diverse campus population. By joining athletic teams, civic organizations and a local women's group, I not only learned how to communicate with non-scientists, but gained a balanced perspective of the role of technology in everyday life. This knowledge is essential in my current position at Myers & Herbst, which is a Wall Street law firm that specializes in patent protection and technology law. Here, I have found a way to bridge my newfound communication skills with my passion for software development.

As fascinated as I am by computer technologies, I am equally captivated by the laws that govern them. Without patent protection, many inventions and theories would not have been developed, because there would have been little incentive to innovate without a guarantee of profit. A legal career will allow me to participate in the protection of technology and intellectual property that deliver so much good to the world. I am also fascinated by the wider realm of international patent protection and the effects it will have on both American companies trying to protect their inventions and emerging economies as they struggle to develop within these confines.

As a paralegal, I have discovered that the law provides an audience that is interested in technology's impact well beyond the laboratory. Increasingly, I have concluded that lawyers employ an even more rigorous standard for truth than scientists, which is an excellent fit for my technical background. Just as in science, the unexpected ambiguities and unanswerable questions of the law constantly keep things interesting.

Although the study of law will require a different kind of thinking, the analytical skills that I cultivated in college will undoubtedly serve me well in law school. Looking ahead, I am excited about the prospects of taking a software company public and securing patent protection for a new pharmaceutical that can cure AIDS. Both are possible in my lifetime. As I prepare to enroll in law school, I feel that I am beginning a career transition that is ripe with opportunities and challenges. I am eager to employ all of my skills, including those of a communicator, to the legal aspects of technology. XXX Law School is the ideal place for my transformation to begin.

Our Assessment: By making fun of the stereotypical image of scientists, this candidate showed the committee that she had a sense of humor about how she was perceived – and that she had taken tangible steps to dispel that image and become an excellent communicator. Her interest in intellectual property law was an excellent fit for her background and skills.

Scientists / Engineers (Part-time JD/MBA program)

By applying a combination of technical and interpersonal strengths, I have advanced to a position as a

Senior Software Engineer in the burgeoning US software and telecommunications industries. After completing my degree in Electronic Engineering at the University of London, I joined Bell South in 2000 as a Technical Solution Specialist. I received several other job offers, but Bell South, which is known for its commercialization of ADSL and ISDN technologies, impressed me with its reputation and expertise. Our corporate objective is to provide software and business solutions to large wire-line and wireless telephone operating companies around the world. In my initial assignment, I worked on a three-member team to resolve business and technical problems after the deployment of a solution. We teamed with the customer's own support staff, which allowed us to build trust and achieve maximum accountability.

Within six months, I was promoted to Software Engineer in the fast growing wireless division, where I design and implement customer-focused solutions. Since my recent promotion to Senior Software Engineer, I have assumed responsibility for the overall coordination of a major project for one of our largest customers. In this capacity, I determined our client's requirements and designed a system to accommodate them. On a daily basis, I serve as the liaison with developers, system engineers, product testers and release managers. I am directly responsible for resource allocation, manpower coordination as well as answering questions from team members and customers. Besides our technical issues, my primary challenges are communicating effectively with my team and coordinating the timing of our work.

With my engineering background, I feel well prepared to handle the technical challenges of project management in the highly competitive telecommunications industry. I can efficiently assess my client's needs and design a solution to suit them. Yet I am increasingly eager to understand the legal and financial needs of my clients in order to help them become more profitable. As I progress in my career, I will need to evaluate the legal implications of developing, marketing and selling new products on a global basis. To develop this expertise, I must balance my technical strengths with formal training in business and the law.

After I complete my JD/MBA, I hope to become an attorney for a large technology firm, where I will use my language fluencies, multicultural experience, technical expertise and business acumen to improve profitability and develop new markets. Ultimately, I hope to become a CEO for a global technology firm, where I will manage change in an increasingly complex world economy.

The flexible scheduling of NYU's program will enable me to acquire a top-notch education while I continue to advance in my current field. As a multilingual professional with international work experience, I will bring a unique perspective to the program. In return, students and faculty members from different industries will provide novel viewpoints and problem-solving techniques. After enjoying the vibrancy and cultural richness of London, I am eager to embrace the same attributes in New York City. I am ready to join the dynamic educational community at NYU.

Our Assessment: This candidate had significant experience in the telecommunications industry, including more than a dozen patents for new technologies that his team had developed. He also had considerable experience managing people, projects, and resources, which allowed him to ascend the ladder in a global technology firm. In this statement, the candidate briefly explains his decision to pursue a joint JD/MBA on a part-time basis while he continues his rapid career trajectory. To the school that accepted him, he offered a rare combination of academic strength, maturity, and professional focus.

Scientists / Engineers

Knowing my passion for crime novels, my family and friends have assumed that my law school aspirations were based on my desire to become a criminal attorney. Initially, the idea did not please my parents, who always envisioned that their talented daughter would become an engineer or a physician. Unbeknownst to them, I entered my university studies in immunology with no inclination towards medicine. Although bacteria, viruses and parasites were "cool" to learn about, I was actually more intrigued by cloned sheep and test tube babies. Now in my graduating year, biotechnology remains my principle field of interest.

Twenty years ago, the idea of selling human embryos in an "underground" market was the stuff of James Bond novels, yet the possibility is no longer simply science fiction. Even nations that support stem cell research, such as China, have seen the development of such a market, which has created a conflict of interest between the urban facilities and rural clinics that supply human embryos. The resolution of these conflicts, and the eventual commercialization of the underlying technologies, will inevitably be resolved in groundbreaking legal cases across the globe. My motivation to attend law school is to lend my voice to the decisions that are made, which will affect not only the future of science but the quality and extension of human life.

My interest in biotechnology was piqued in high school, when I wrote my senior thesis on the bioethics of reproductive technologies. In my subsequent years at the University of London, the topic has grown in controversy with the explosion of stem cell research. My studies in immunology have given me the flexibility to learn about diseases, germs, and their applications in biotechnology while simultaneously exploring other fields that allow me to view my scientific knowledge within a global context.

As a college freshman, I got my first taste of the global impact of biotechnology at the University's summit on genomics and biotechnology. Last year, I was a member of a pioneer group that established the school's first student-run bioethics conference. Despite the amazing possibilities and implications, I discovered that few people seemed to possess adequate knowledge about the booming biotechnology industry. From my perspective, there is compelling need to take this knowledge to the general public to initiate a dialogue about the underlying moral, ethical, and legal issues.

After the success of the first bioethics conference, we decided to expand the event for 2011. As this year's chair, I am fulfilling our vision of an international conference, which is attracting delegates and speakers from South Korea, India, the Philippines and the United States. Our participants are not just scientists, but internationally recognized experts in medicine, law, business, philosophy, sociology and religion, who will evaluate the issues from a 360-degree angle in diverse academic, social and cultural contexts. By widening the demographic of the conference, we hope to increase awareness and stimulate debate of not only the controversial "hot topics," such as stem cell research, but of lesser discussed (but equally fascinating) issues such as organ transplants, aging, and various forms of life enhancement and extension.

The intense competition in this technologically-driven society has created an unprecedented need for laws to govern and protect the very innovations that feed it. In addition to appreciating the moral rationale of an issue, legal professionals must understand the embedded technical jargon in order to avoid misconceptions that influence the ratification of regulations that impede scientific progress. In the global village, nations such as China, South Korea, the UK and the US are competing to maintain their positions as world leaders on the frontiers of biotechnological research and development. With my multicultural background, I will be well positioned to satisfy the demand for scientifically savvy legal professionals who can bridge the gap between disparate cultures. At XXX Law School, I will acquire the expertise in international intellectual property law that will enable me to contribute to the legal needs of a blossoming biotechnology industry.

Our Assessment: This strength of this statement is that it explores the candidate's long-term interest in biotechnology, including her participation in global conferences on topics such as stem cell research, organ transplantation, and cloning. Her insight into the moral and legal implications of new technologies was an excellent fit for the programs that accepted her.

Artists, Writers & Musicians

It is ironic that one of the best universities in the nation is located in a racially and socio-economically segregated community where more than 50% of the children drop out of high school and fewer than 10% attend college. The startling contrast between the peaceful oasis of the Yale University campus and the urban blight of the surrounding community has always been unsettling to me. At 18, I decided to try to integrate the two communities by starting an after-school music program at the nearby New Haven Family Center. After teaching violin classes at a charter school in Boston, I was confident that I could establish a similar program in New Haven. Coming from Philips Academy, a well-endowed preparatory school, I had forgotten the importance of funding in launching such an ambitious volunteer venture. Without the generosity of wealthy donors and alumni, I had to be much more creative to get the New Haven String Program off the ground.

Fortunately, I have always been passionate about sharing the power of music. After my birth in Los Angeles in 1986, I enjoyed a privileged childhood in which my parents encouraged me to pursue my athletic and artistic talents. When I was 4 years old, my family moved to Japan, where I explored my interests in languages, piano and violin. Later, in grade 10, I followed in my brother's footsteps and decided to study in the United States. Ironically, although I was born in the US, I found myself reluctant to leave the familiarity of Japan. Unlike my previous relocation, when everything seemed exciting and new, I was ambivalent about living in a strange place that required a 20-hour journey across 8,000 miles and twelve time zones.

The environment at Philips Academy, which is a boarding school in the suburbs, was dramatically different than the hustle and bustle of a cosmopolitan city like Tokyo. Although I struggled with my initial adjustment, I quickly came to enjoy the benefits of my independence. At Philips Academy, I was no longer under my parents' supervision; I was able to pick the courses that I liked and choose the activities that I wanted to do. As a result, I learned how to manage my time, to be independent, and to be disciplined. Moreover, I had the opportunity to meet "youth from every quarter" and to make several lifelong friends. On both an academic and personal level, Philips Academy helped me to prepare for the challenges of college.

When I evaluated universities, I focused on places where I could get a global education with a healthy balance of the sciences, arts, and humanities. Then, I differentiated the schools based on non-academic factors, including my personal fit with the people and culture. The minute I stepped onto the Yale campus, I sensed a feeling of familiarity. The neo-gothic buildings, the green quads, and the wide-spreading trees brought back happy memories of my years at Philips Academy. In addition, the close-knit student body and the intimate feeling on campus quickly captured my heart. I knew that Yale was the best place for me to learn and grow.

In hindsight, starting the New Haven String Program was the most rewarding aspect of my undergraduate experience, because it integrated my love of music with my interest in community development. In our seemingly segregated world, music has the power to quiet our differences and bring a sense of unity to a roomful of strangers. Amazingly, a well-run music program also attracts the interest of numerous talented participants. Within a few weeks, the New Haven String Program had generated enthusiasm among hundreds of musicians on campus; to my delight, it also attracted dozens of aspiring performers from our local public high schools, who were searching for an opportunity to showcase their talents. The program's ability to bring these groups together – and to cultivate talent and relationships simultaneously, has given me the confidence to pursue a career as an advocate for social change.

Through the New Haven String Program, our volunteers brought a musical gift to inner-city students and served as ambassadors of goodwill across these communities. The children learned to genuinely appreciate music, and came to perceive our campus as being open with possibilities instead of elitist and closed to them. I discovered, on a deeply personal level, that one person can make a tangible difference in building a sense of community between disparate groups of people. This spirit of optimism inspires me to utilize my experiences and skills to help others who do not have the access to opportunities that I have always taken for granted.

Our Assessment: Although not perfect, this essay conveys the candidate's leadership skills in a clear and persuasive way. It also conveyed her lifelong passion for music, which she shared with others through the New Haven String Program. A year later, the candidate launched a similar group at the law school where she subsequently enrolled.

Artists, Writers & Musicians

As I shook his hand, I was dazzled by his bright smile and clear, sparkling eyes. For a brief second, I was overwhelmed by the charisma that Bill Clinton effortlessly exudes. After he thanked me for my work on his campaign, he enraptured the crowd with his plans for the country. Twenty years later, Bill Clinton remains a true American hero who is one of the greatest legal minds of the twentieth century. He is the reason that I have faith in my country and am willing to take risks; I know that my hard work, dedication and perseverance will pay off.

Public policy has always been my passion. As a college student, my proudest achievement was the successful organization of the "Rock the Vote" rally at Yale University, which was sponsored by political activist Michael Moore, a staunch supporter of then-candidate Bill Clinton. As chapter president of the Yale Democrats, I wrote several letters and editorials on Clinton's behalf for publication in the *New York Times*. In my senior year, three of my columns were syndicated in papers across London and Germany.

Following graduation, I converted my interest in writing into a successful journalism career with *USA Today*. By design, I assume challenges that the mainstream press avoids. Under my auspices, *USA Today* published a series of articles called the "Diverse Spectrum," which documented a number of controversial race-related issues in Connecticut politics that had been ignored by the mainstream press. As expected, the series generated healthy debate among our readers, which sparked an investigation into state hiring practices by the ACLU.

I am also the author of a weekly column called "Political Leanings," which features in-depth interviews with little-known political candidates who lack the funds to get their voices heard. A year ago, I expanded my journalistic portfolio by accepting a position as co-host of "Yankee Voices," a political radio call-in show in New Haven. By combining careful research and an engaging presentation style, I bring my audience compelling political information during their morning drive.

My goal is to lead the intellectual exchange of political information on a global level, as a senior manager of a communications firm. I want to present and explain political issues to a wider audience than the readers of *USA Today*. Although we live in a democracy, few citizens consider political issues to be an instructive force in their lives. The more they know, the better they can execute their responsibilities as citizens, both inside and outside the voting booth.

As I advance in my career as a political journalist, I am increasingly aware of the "hidden agenda" behind what is reported in the news. Most of what the public "knows" is not necessarily fact, but the ruminations of a biased source. The huge corporations that own most US magazines, newspapers and television stations are not motivated by a commitment to the truth, but by the edicts of a CEO and corporate board with an agenda all their own. My goal is to bring an unbiased perspective to the executive leadership of an international news organization.

Why Yale? Because it's the best university in the world. My success as a journalist is primarily due to the critical thinking skills I acquired in your undergraduate program in communications. I am grateful to the faculty's insistence that I question the status quo and develop my own values. Yale's commitment to open discussions will facilitate a creative exchange of ideas among the eclectic student body. As a seasoned political journalist, I will contribute my unique perspective of the long-term economic implications of domestic and international politics. The time is right for me to advance in my field and direct the content of news for the next generation. I can't imagine a better place to prepare for this objective than at Yale.

Our Assessment: This is an exceptional essay from an exceptional candidate. By explaining his early interest in politics – and his memorable meeting with Bill Clinton – he captured the reader's interest in the first line and retained it until the very end. His accomplishments as a journalist and political editor were particularly well perceived.

Social Services

As a social worker for the city of Detroit, I am committed to rebuilding our city and banishing illegal drugs from our streets. That isn't simply idealistic rhetoric. For the past twelve years, I have fought vigilantly to protect our poor and neglected children whose parents are drug addicts. It's a stressful - and often thankless - job that is huge in scope and sometimes unbearably painful. Yet my motivation is inherently personal. I believe that the social workers who intervened with my family literally saved my life.

I was born to a single mother in South Detroit and lived alone with her in an abandoned old building. My mother was mentally ill and began to disappear from our room for extensive periods of time. Finally, when I was 4, she disappeared for good. I was taken by a social worker named Mary to an intake facility and subjected to the first physical exam of my life. Mary stayed with me while her colleagues scrubbed my lean black arms and pulled dozens of lice from my head. For three long months, I lived in a county rehab facility where I was fed, clothed and taught to live as a functioning human being.

For several years, I was the poster child for the "hard to place" adoptee. Yet, miraculously, I was taken in by an older African American couple who were up to the challenge of raising an abandoned, hyperactive 7-year-old boy. Joe and Vivian Fox loved me unconditionally from the moment our eyes met and they gave me the only home that I have ever known. I lived with them until I graduated from college and I still consider them my family. I will always be grateful for their love, support, and nurturance in my life.

In my darkest moments, I ponder where I would be if the social workers had not been called to rescue me from that abandoned building. I could easily have died from neglect, starvation or a violent encounter. I might never have found a home, attended school or had a chance for a normal life. No one knows how many other kids are living in equally dire circumstances. We have a serious problem with societal breakdown in our inner cities that must be exposed, assessed and solved.

After college, I returned to South Detroit to work as a social worker. The problems are as severe as I remember, yet I am committed to being part of the solution. My position as a case worker for the Department of Human Services requires me to intervene in situations that are very similar to the ones I endured as a young boy. I remove children from dangerous and neglectful situations that usually originate from their parents' addictions. Although we always try to repair the original family unit, that is usually not possible. Parents die, are imprisoned, or do not want to reclaim their children. Happy endings are rare.

When I feel overwhelmed by my job, I am inspired by Mary, my mentor and role model. After all these years, she is still working at Social Services to make our city a better place. Mary personalizes a system that is notorious for being overworked and detached. I'm not sure that the Department of Human Services realizes the rare gem that they have in her.

Mary and I often discuss the best way to solve the problems in Detroit. With a law degree, I will be able to write successful grant proposals, develop programs and lobby for money. I also plan to acquire the communication skills I will need to articulate our needs to the lawmakers who represent us in Congress. Most of our benefactors lack the personal perspective that I have acquired from growing up in the system. They don't understand the root problems. From my work, I know our critical needs and how to approach them. After law school, I want to rise to a position that will allow me to allocate our limited resources where they will make the most difference. Although I cannot save the world, I am committed to doing my part.

Our Assessment: This essay, although long and imperfect, tells an honest and heartfelt story of this candidate's journey from abandonment to social servant. His recommendation letters, which documented his long and accomplished career path, gave the committee further confirmation of his motivation and character.

Social Services

As the dilapidated Jeep made its way along the dirt road, I finally caught a glimpse of the lush African landscape. Our destination was Jutta, a tiny village two hundred miles north of Zambia, where telephones, running water and electricity were completely unavailable. As a freshman at Duke University, I was part of a multinational team that was spending the summer in Africa on a medical development project. The trip to Jutta was my first jaunt outside the United States, much less to a third world area. For a brief second on that dirt road, I wondered if I had been kidding myself about my ability to make a difference in the world.

Fortunately, once we reached the makeshift clinic, we managed to establish a moderate degree of normalcy. From eight o'clock each morning until six o'clock in the evening, we treated a long line of patients who arrived on foot, on horseback and on motorbike from the surrounding villages. For many, we were the only medical professionals they had ever seen. My pseudo professionalism melted when I heard their tragic stories. One afternoon, a young woman arrived with her sick infant after trekking nearly ten miles to reach us. She was not lactating effectively, and her child lay emaciated and dying. As I administered fluids to the baby, I was amazed by my ability to make a tangible difference in their lives.

Although I did not choose to enroll in law school immediately after college, my desire to work in public health has never waned during my subsequent decade of academic, professional, and volunteer experiences. Armed with a BA in Biology and a MS in Public Health Services, I have pursued many diverse experiences to improve the availability of health care services on a worldwide basis. Each activity has strengthened my conviction that I can make a meaningful contribution to people's lives on both the individual and societal level. Moreover, I am confident that my various experiences will help me to be a broader, more informed, and more sensitive attorney.

At Georgetown University, where I have taught classes in Public Health Policy for the past six years, my interest in cross-cultural communication drew me to study the relationships between medicine, the law and politics. These variables play a key role in determining a nation's commitment to public service, particularly regarding women's health issues. My studies taught me that improved infrastructure and health education might have prevented many of the conditions that we had treated in Africa. I acted on my concerns by working with the U.S. State Department in Zambia and Ghana, where I gained firsthand insight into policy formation.

But I also acknowledged a profound limitation; to help people in a direct and tangible way, I need a law degree. Without support at the international level, programs such as the one I championed in Zambia and Ghana will cease to exist. After law school, I hope to become a voice of hope for underserved regions, whose people cannot survive without the intervention of quality medical care and education. This spring, I will return to Zambia with Hope 2012, which is an outreach group from Georgetown, to establish rural health clinics on the outskirts of Jutta. I see my three-month commitment as an opportunity to bring short-term care to an underserved area that deserves a voice in the fledgling African health care system.

After I complete my law degree, I will continue to work for groups like Hope 2012, which are committed to developing viable health care policies in emerging areas. Fifteen years after my first memorable trip to Zambia, I am excited to finally fulfill my destiny by obtaining my law degree. The skills I have acquired through research, policy analysis, volunteer work and cross-cultural interaction will enable me to make a meaningful contribution to the communities I serve.

Our Assessment: This statement, although long, reveals the author's distinguished record as a public health advocate. She was a welcome addition to the program that admitted her, which specializes in this area.

Social Services

Despite the pressure of my job, I have retained the idealism that inspired me to become a social worker for the city of Baton Rouge. My goal is to remove abused and neglected children from bad situations and get them the resources they need to lead successful and fulfilling lives. As an interviewer, I have learned how to ask the "tough" questions to get the information I need. More importantly, I have learned that it is what a person *isn't* saying that actually defines the problem and suggests the most appropriate solution. I feel blessed to have excellent listening skills, which can only be cultivated by the proper combination of temperament and experience. No class can teach you to care about people or to go that extra mile to look inside their hearts.

My most challenging case confirmed my decision to pursue a career in the law. It began as a typical abuse/negligence investigation in the industrial section of Wesley. We received several anonymous tips that a young African-American boy was roaming a condemned building at all hours of the night. He was a charming rogue who was eager to speak to strangers and ask for spare change. The boy was cagey, though, and careful to conceal his name. After speaking to him several times, our callers suspected that he was homeless and possibly abandoned.

I approached the collapsing building with trepidation, not knowing who or what was inside. Wishing that I had a burly partner, I immediately came face-to-face with a little boy who called himself Josh. I found him alone in a stiflingly hot room with his grievously ill mother, Sonya. Just six years old, Josh would beg for food all day and bring it back for his mother. I can't begin to describe the family's horrible living environment. Since the building had no running water, neither Josh nor Sonya had bathed or changed clothes for weeks.

When the police brought Sonya to the hospital, we discovered that she was in the final stages of AIDS and had zero chance for survival. Although I moved onto my next case, I couldn't erase Josh or Sonya from my mind. I placed Josh with a foster family that had the patience to work with a child who suffered from severe neglect. I also visited Sonya in the hospital; I learned that she was a 23-year-old prostitute and heroin addict who could neither read nor write. She had given birth to three children, but only Josh had survived more than a few days. Despite her dire symptoms, Sonya had not visited a doctor since before Josh was born.

Sadly, I had heard the details of her story hundreds of times before. Sonya is one of thousands of women in our city who have fallen through the cracks of our medical and social service systems, yet she touched me in a way I never dreamed possible. Before she met me, Sonya had no way to cut through the bureaucracy and find the services she needed to save herself or her son. As a result, she was never treated for the illness that killed her and made Josh an orphan. A legal education will enable me to become an advocate in this area and possibly save other families from the plight that Sonya endured.

Following graduation, I plan to champion the types of intervention that can save people like Josh and Sonya, such as preventive programs in drug abuse, AIDS awareness, and training in basic life skills. I will lobby for job training programs, day care centers and a vastly improved community infrastructure to serve our citizens. A law degree will add to my skill set in a way that benefits not just my own professional advancement, but that of the community. I owe it to the women like Sonya, who died needlessly at far too early an age.

Our Assessment: This is a powerful statement from a social worker who had spent more than a decade trying to help vulnerable populations. By telling the story about Sonya and Josh, he revealed his passion, character, and leadership skills, which made a positive impact on the committee.

Older Candidate - International Entrepreneurship

After the civil wars in Colombia, I worked as a volunteer for the Red Cross, Save the Children, and other relief groups that provided food, water and medical care throughout the remote regions of the country. In 2007, I started a business to help restore the essential infrastructure to support telephone and internet service. After several years of active solicitation, I convinced an American company to invest in Colombia. Through my company, Sprint now provides telephone and internet service to most of the nation. We are currently negotiating a merger with a US company, which will allow us to operate in Argentina and Brazil. Our presence in these nations will radically alter the price-structure in the telecommunications industry, where one hour of internet access currently costs 10 US dollars. Acknowledging the power of the internet and real-time access to information, our goal is to provide the cheapest telecommunications service in South America.

My venture has faced continual challenges at each stage of its development. Finding initial investors was impossible, because no one wanted to invest in a war-ridden nation. The representatives from Sprint agreed to visit our office only if we paid the cost for their private security. In our first year of business, we lost considerable revenue due to prolonged, unexpected power outages throughout the region. Although we initially thought that the electric company was sabotaging us, we later discovered that the telephone lines were severely damaged from prolonged periods of disrepair. No one in authority was willing to invest in their restoration without a financial incentive from us. Through artful negotiations, I agreed to subsidize a portion of the repairs in return for a price break from the electric company on our services. In most countries, this would be called a bribe; in Colombia, it's simply the way we do business.

My most serious challenges were related to safety. After the United Nations sent their peacekeeping forces, it took a full year before the general public actually felt safe. My customers were hesitant to go outside, much less invest money in a computer and internet connection. I solved this problem by providing exceptional private security at our internet cafes, which I advertised aggressively. I also began a massive public relations campaign to educate the public about what the internet could do for them, both personally and professionally. Although we lost money during our first two years, by the time the market recovered, we were the only ones in the region who provided safe, reliable, economical service. Consequently, we became the brand of choice for both telephone and internet service. And, by playing it safe, our competitors lost two valuable years in trying to penetrate the market.

When I look back over my considerable progress, I attribute my success chiefly to my unwavering perseverance. Despite all evidence to the contrary, I never considered any obstacle to be life-threatening. Through negotiation, flexibility and well-developed contingency plans, I established several strategic partnerships to achieve my goals. Even in the bleakest moments, I never gave up. My future success as an international business attorney will undoubtedly hinge on these same intrinsic strengths.

Our Assessment: This candidate used the statement as a platform to present her most compelling accomplishment – launching a successful business in a war-torn nation. By explaining the process to the reader, she revealed her motivation, initiative, and problem solving skills, which made a tremendous impression on the admissions committee.

Older Candidate - Sales

"You would make a great lawyer." Despite the abundance of jokes about the legal profession, I have learned to take this remark as a compliment. After all, as a successful sales consultant, I have developed many of the same skills I will use as a litigator. I am a careful listener, an articulate speaker and a skilled negotiator. By surviving several personal setbacks, I have become a persistent woman who can solve tough problems. I also have a passionate interest in defending the rights of people who do not have a voice. Consequently, when I envision my future, I am confident that the legal profession is my destiny.

As a child, the thought of becoming an attorney in the United States seemed like an impossible dream. My family moved from Tokyo to Boston when I was just ten years old. Although I didn't speak a word of English, my parents always told me that I could accomplish anything. Their words became a powerful mantra, "By working hard and getting an education, you can handle any challenge that comes your way." Eventually, I realized that they were correct. With persistence and determination, I graduated in the top 10% of my high school class and completed two bachelor's degrees and a master's degree in just six years. Thanks to my parents' nurturance, I developed the confidence to take the necessary risks to achieve my dreams.

After completing my formal education in Operations Research, I pursued a successful career in the enterprise software industry. For the past twelve years, I have excelled in my work as a technology sales consultant at Zenith Software, where I help my customers find technical solutions to their business problems. My primary challenge is to ask the "right" questions to determine their need; then, I must explain a complex solution in an understandable way. I am blessed with the right combination of temperament and skills to help my clients realize the value of the technology that I provide. As a result, I have qualified for the top tier quota club for eleven years, missing only during the time that I was on maternity leave.

Looking back, my role in technical sales provided the initial spark for my interest in a legal career. Unlike most fields, the technology sector develops new products in a matter of weeks or months. At any point in time, revolutionary technology can emerge and totally change the competitive landscape. In addition, many of the products it develops can be pirated easily. As I progress in the field, I am captivated by the legal challenges that plague my industry, particularly the disputes relating to intellectual property rights and antitrust issues. With a law degree, I can use my technical knowledge and expertise to help individual and corporate clients resolve the complex legal challenges relating to these issues. My cultural background and language capability will be especially helpful in dealing with intellectual property disputes between the US and Japan.

My second motivation to study law is personal. When my marriage ended in 2006, I faced considerable resistance from my abusive husband, who tried to prevent me from obtaining a divorce. Throughout the two years of court proceedings, I was frustrated by the prolonged delays and voluminous paperwork needed to cut through the legal "red tape." In my darkest hours, I devoured the Massachusetts Family Code to learn how to protect my rights and those of my daughter. Thankfully, I am one of the fortunate ones; I have a supportive family and a thriving career. Since then, I have met many women through my volunteer work who did not have the economic resources to live on their own or to obtain protection from the court system. Once I am licensed to practice law, I plan to take pro-bono cases to help abused women build better lives for themselves and their children.

When I evaluated prospective law schools, Boston University immediately emerged as my first choice. First, it has a strong academic reputation in intellectual property law, which is my primary interest. Second, I value the school's corporate ties to Boston's telecommunications corridor and the reputation it carries in the community. Third, with my strong family connection in Boston, I am proud to call the city "home." I have lived in many wonderful places, but my heart always remains in Massachusetts. After I graduate from law school, I plan to help build a safer and more vibrant community.

At age 40, I know that I face a dramatic change in lifestyle to enroll in law school, yet I am committed to this goal. After twenty years of diverse educational and professional experiences, I am certain that a legal career is my destiny.

Our Assessment: This is an exceptional statement from an exceptional candidate. Her dual passion for family law and intellectual property law showed the committee her depth and maturity, which were highly prized in the admissions process. As an added bonus, the candidate targeted schools that valued the specific strengths she had to offer; she was a perfect match for the university in Massachusetts that accepted her.

Older Candidate - Experience in Law Enforcement

As I prepared for work, I got the type of call that every investigator dreads. A girl's body had been found behind a Montessori pre-school and I was needed at the scene. By the time I arrived, the victim had been covered with a sheet and my colleagues were conducting an area search for any clues to her identity. At that point, no one knew who she was, how she died or who might have been responsible. Before the students began to arrive at the school, we needed to process the scene and take her body to the morgue.

During my ten years as a crime investigator, I never got used to death. As I arrived at the Medical Examiner's Office, I took a moment to begin the initial stage of my investigation. Considering the victim's age, I knew the case would be difficult. Losing children always was. As I walked into the autopsy room, I was moved by the petite body of an Asian girl who was only fifteen years old. I didn't know her name, but I recognized her Avia sneakers as being identical to those of my daughter. As I conferred with the M.E., I couldn't shake the awful thought that she could have *been* my daughter.

As the M.E. carefully examined every organ, I documented his findings in my notebook. An immediate clue was that the victim had been raped, which could help us to determine who had beaten her to death and dumped her body behind the pre-school. Through my investigation, I learned that the victim (Ling Li) had been orphaned by a car accident that killed both of her parents. Afterwards, she was sexually abused by her only remaining relative, who had been convicted of the charges and sent to state prison. Since then, Ling Li had been placed in several foster homes, but she never seemed to fit in. Her last family, which hadn't seen Ling Li in two months, didn't even bother to report her missing.

As a parent, I was chilled by the callous manner in which Ling Li had been passed from home to home without getting her needs met. I was particularly saddened to learn that she had participated in our department's formal mentoring program for troubled teens. Suddenly, her case became personal to me. Despite my efforts to keep teenagers safe, Ling Li had fallen through the cracks. I was determined to give her the type of help that had eluded her during her short life.

Fortunately, we solved the case due to the miraculous specificity of DNA testing. For several weeks, I meticulously prepared lab reports and DNA profiles on the blood, swabs, cultures and fibers that we recovered from the scene. After several days, the County Crime Laboratory answered my prayers; they had made a DNA match. The killer was a repeat offender who had been back on the streets for less than a month at the time of Ling Li's death. Thanks to our work, he was convicted of her murder and sentenced to 45 years to life.

Many times, when they learn of my career, people ask me why I am committed to such a stressful job. The victims and their families keep me going, long after most would give up. In every case, I respect each victim, regardless of how and why (s)he died. I also assure their family members that we will do everything in our power to bring closure to such a difficult time in their lives. For many victims, like Ling Li, it is the only time that someone is willing to fight for their honor. Better late than not at all…….

Our Assessment: This candidate struggled with several themes before she drafted this essay, which spoke directly from the heart. By telling the story of this investigation, she showed the committee how important the victim was to her – and the amazing work that she did to bring her killer to justice.

Older Candidate with Advanced Degree

The sea is a continual miracle. The fishes that swim....the rocks....the motion of the waves....... What stranger miracles are there?

                 -- Walt Whitman ""*Miracles*" 1856

As a young child, I spent every summer fishing and swimming at the beach in Rhode Island. Everything about the sea seemed ethereal to me: its foamy waves, translucent color, and simultaneous ability to nurture and threaten non-marine life. In stressful times, the ocean provided more than simply a source of recreation; it offered the peace and respite from city life that I desperately craved.

Over the years, I noticed that the shoreline and fish supply began to diminish in equal measure. My desire to understand (and possibly reverse) these phenomena inspired my college major in marine biology. I couldn't imagine a more fulfilling use of my scientific knowledge than to preserve the natural resources that I had spent a lifetime enjoying. As an undergraduate student, I pursued several opportunities to work in the field; I maintained the animals and husbandry facilities at the Rhode Island State Aquarium and I supervised offshore field trips for several high school groups. I subsequently earned my B.S. in Marine Biology from the University of Rhode Island and an M.S. in Fisheries and Allied Aquacultures from the University of Massachusetts at Amherst.

Following my masters degree, I completed three years of coursework toward a Ph.D. in Fisheries and Allied Aquacultures. As a graduate research assistant, I published my findings and made formal presentations at meetings for the Aquaculture Society, the National Shellfish Association and the American Fisheries Society. Despite my success in the field, I recognized that I would never be truly fulfilled by pursuing a career in teaching or research. Instead, I wanted to use my knowledge to protect our food supply from the ongoing threat of human and industrial contamination.

My most recent project investigated ways to minimize the impact of aquaculture on the environment, particularly effluent discharge and water pollution. Amazingly, at my last national meeting, I was the only attendee who understood its advantages over commercial fisheries, which are dangerous, labor intensive, and energy inefficient. Even worse, they leave harmful contaminants in the ocean than affect the quality of the fish and the safety of the beaches for swimmers and boaters. While researching these issues, I recognized the need for specialists who understand the technical, legal, environmental, and economic aspects of aquaculture, which will improve the quality of our food supply and the purity of the ocean. My primary motivation for attending law school is to acquire this expertise. Combined with my research experience and my extensive knowledge of marine biology, a law degree will enable me to resolve complex legal and environmental issues regarding fishing and aquaculture in a beneficial way.

I am particularly interested in Georgetown University because of its strong reputation in environmental law. In addition, its close proximity to Washington, DC offers a rare opportunity for me to work with federal groups that champion relevant legislation. A legal education will enable me to assume a unique niche in the profession by promoting environmental concerns from a scientific perspective. With my help, future generations will continue to enjoy the beauty of Rhode Island's coastline in the pristine form it was created. I am honored to heed this calling.

Our Assessment: As a general rule, you should only open your statement with a quotation if it is directly related to your actual topic. This candidate took that risk and it paid off. In a short space, he explains his unique motivation for becoming an attorney, which was a perfect match for his educational background. The statement was well perceived.

Career Switch

I stood in front of the brightly lit Christmas tree, trying to keep my teeth from chattering in the sub-zero weather. As we waited to film the "beauty shot" that would close the news broadcast, I tried to muster some holiday cheer. As the newest female reporter at the station, I inherited most of the lighter "fluff" pieces that ended our broadcasts. It was a true entry-level position. On any given day, I might film a cat show, high school spelling bee or a Halloween pumpkin carving competition. Although I appreciated my chance to work in front of the camera, I longed to spread my wings and report more challenging stories.

With my station manager's blessing, I filmed a few legal spots as part of our community awareness program. They were not particularly deep - just practical advice on how to deal with landlords, noisy neighbors, botched home repairs and "lemon"-quality appliances. Thankfully, they received such a positive reception that I was asked to work on more substantial pieces. In February of 2008, I ran an interview with State Attorney Steven Collins, who had successfully prosecuted several high-profile child abuse cases. Following our piece, which highlighted the early warning signs of child abuse, we received over 400 requests for additional information. I was touched by the support of the community and their obvious interest in protecting the rights of children.

Thankfully, viewers encouraged us to keep airing the legal segments, so I began to air a weekly in-depth interview about relevant issues in our community. In late 2009, I investigated water pollution from a local manufacturing plant, elderly abuse in a nursing home, and tainted meat in a fast-food restaurant. In each piece, I featured our local State Attorney, who summarized the state's role in trying to protect the public.

As I learned more about the legal profession, I envied the ability of Steven Collins to protect the public interest. I also enjoyed flexing my investigative skills. My reporting experience reminded me that my initial career goal was actually to become a lawyer. After two years of humanities classes, I started to work at the campus television station and fell in love with broadcasting. With little thought, I switched to a communications degree and traded my case studies and legal pads for a microphone.

In hindsight, the choice was not inherently bad. I landed a position in a growing market and had every reason to believe that I could become successful. Who would have guessed that I would be unfulfilled as a "talking head?" By 2009, my weekly legal pieces were my lifeline to a satisfying career. I could no longer deny that law school was the answer.

As I consider my career transition, I am amazed by how many skills are common to both broadcasting and the law. With each case, attorneys are investigators and reporters in their own right, as they gather evidence to convince a jury of a suspect's guilt. They utilize many of the same skills as a journalist, with the added challenge of adhering to the law. I am intrigued by the challenge.

My close friends cannot understand why I am making this change, considering the hard work and dedication that I have invested in my current career. While I enjoy working as a "talking head," I cannot ignore my desire to make a more significant contribution to my community. Hopefully, in ten years, I will be a prosecutor like Steven Collins, who makes the streets a little bit safer for everyone else. The next time I'm photographed in front of a Christmas tree, I'm hoping that it will be at Princeton, surrounded by my fellow members of my law school class.

Our Assessment: This candidate is a famous journalist who left her career to pursue a law degree. In this statement, she explains the reasons for that change in an informative and eloquent way.

Career Switch

On September 11, 2001, my only class that remained in session was *Beginning Arabic*. As I scanned the classroom, which was filled with numerous Arab-American students, I saw fear and sadness in the eyes of my peers. As the students spoke, their voices trembled with emotion. They were concerned about retaliation against their family and friends in the Middle East, and even for themselves. Our professor, who was originally from Palestine, had been assaulted that morning by a student at the university. Still shaken from the day's events, he mediated the students' discussion with quiet dignity. His traditional Palestinian headdress, which he always wore with pride, gently cloaked his shoulders.

As a journalism student, I felt compelled to write about the incidents that followed the September 11 tragedy. My professor's humiliating assault was entrenched in my mind as I interviewed Sikh and non-Muslim South Asian students. Many of them were harassed by shouts of "bin Laden" as they walked across campus, the same discrimination that was aimed at anyone who could possibly be Arab. I was horrified by these acts of aggression toward my friends, peers and professors. When I wrote my stories, I hoped that my readers would confront the hostility in our community and prevent others from being victimized. Unfortunately, as the world wrestled with fear and sadness, my articles could not stop the misdirected hostility of shell-shocked readers. For several weeks, I questioned my decision to become a political journalist.

The following year, through a scholarship from the State Department, I traveled to the Middle East to continue my studies of the Arabic language. The world was on the brink of war. As my plane touched down in Egypt, there were protests at the American Embassy and on campuses in Cairo. I watched with awe as students and professors abandoned their classes to voice their thoughts in a society that restricts free speech. As I observed the emotional scene, I knew that I must continue to write about world events, regardless of the narrow-minded response in America.

Since December of 2002, I have been a political reporter for the *Advocate*, where I cover the continual unrest that surrounds the US invasion of Iraq. My stories have been simultaneously uplifting and grim, as I report on the injuries inflicted on innocent children and the medical efforts to save them. My 2004 series "Women in Iraq" provided the first in-depth interviews with Iraqi professional women, who are taking their first tentative steps into democracy. As I heard their stories of courage and fear, I yearned to solve their problems, rather than simply write about them.

The September 11 attacks affected every nation, as we struggle with the ongoing threats of terrorism in an uncertain world. My global travel experiences suggest that a legal advocate can bridge the gap between different cultures and create synergy and compromise from ignorance and fear. In retrospect, I chose a journalism career for many reasons; its diversity, immediacy and unparalleled ability to shed light in dark corners. My decision to pursue a legal education is rooted in those same ideals. Reporting on the aftermath of September 11 has compelled me to use my skills to make a difference in the world. As a writer, I bring clarity to devastating world events; as an attorney, I will change their direction.

Our Assessment: This candidate is an accomplished journalist who has won numerous awards for her work. In the statement, she explains how her career trajectory in the aftermath of September 11 affected her decision to become an attorney. Her ability to discuss an emotional topic in an objective was particularly well perceived.

JD/MBA Applicant

Cancer. On the surface, it's simple word: two syllables, six letters, a common term both for a fatal disease and a crab-based astrological sign. Until my freshman year in high school, the word had no particular meaning to me because cancer had not touched my life. Everything changed with a phone call from my pediatrician, informing me that I had a malignancy in my lower bowel. Suddenly, the simple, two-syllable word came to define a grueling regimen of surgery, chemotherapy and radiation to beat the odds and eventually be cured. Six years later, I still view conquering the disease as the most significant achievement of my life.

My battle with illness caused me to reflect on the positive aspects of my fight. In particular, I realized that it was important for me to share my experience with people in similar situations. During the first year of my treatment, I worked as a peer consultant at St. Louis Pediatric Medical Center, where hundreds of other families struggled with same illness. By providing insight and comfort during a difficult period, I gained a more optimistic view of my own situation. In the six years since my original diagnosis, I have continued to volunteer at the Medical Center during my summer vacations, which has confirmed that there is sunshine on the other side of the rainbow.

The strength and independence that came from my battle with cancer carried over to my position as student manager of WKRP, the University of Ohio's 30,000 watt commercial radio station. As a business major, I relished the opportunity to flex my administrative muscles on this promising yet unprofitable venture. My first job was to increase revenue from our 37 advertising accounts. By raising rates and expanding our sales base, I increased our profits by more than 80 percent in my first year, while simultaneously spending over $50,000 for capital improvements. As part of a cost-saving initiative in October 2009, I switched our mail order suppliers, which dramatically increased the cost efficiency of our offices.

To my surprise, the position at WKRP also involved many legal issues. To avoid a costly court battle, I negotiated settlements on the two largest, inherited, overdue accounts. I also redesigned the contracts for our sales representatives and ensured that we followed all FCC regulations. During my senior year of college, I leveraged my business and legal skills to form my own musical entertainment company called Jams Limited. Starting with no employees or capital, I now have five employees, three regional 800 numbers, and clients from Columbus to Chicago. In addition to drafting all of the legal contracts for the firm, I also handle all marketing and promotions. The time commitment to the company is large, but the rewards of running my own entrepreneurial venture makes every minute worthwhile.

My motivation for applying to the joint JD / MBA program is two-fold. First, I am eager to acquire the business and legal expertise I will need to expand my entertainment business on a global level. As rap music increases in popularity, companies that provide live acts in smaller venues will enjoy increased revenues and growth. I want to be prepared to handle all aspects of this expansion. Second, I am eager to establish a non-profit organization to provide free and low-cost wigs to children with cancer. One of the hardest experiences for me was losing my hair in high school. To whatever extent possible, I want to help other children avoid the stress of having such a visible symptom of their disease.

Although I would never have chosen to have cancer, its lessons have propelled me to accomplish as much as possible with my life, wasting neither time nor opportunity. The dual JD/ MBA program at Harvard represents a critical next step in achieving my aggressive, but achievable goals.

Our Assessment: This essay attempts something that is very difficult to do – it combines two themes (cancer and business experience) into a unified whole, to explain the candidate's joint interest in business and the law. Although the flow in the essay is not perfect, the narrative works – and gives the reader keen insight into the tenacity of this amazing young woman.

Managerial Experience: JD/MBA Candidate

A cracked jaw, two broken ribs, and minor scalp abrasions. Chronic back pain of non-specific origin. As I flipped through the patient's file, I wondered how she could possibly have obtained such serious injuries from a fall in our restaurant's kitchen. As a waitress, she walked back and forth from the hallway to the dining area at least a hundred times each day. Why did she fall? The floor was clean and dry, which made her claim of "unsafe conditions" difficult to verify. Yet my job as Operations Manager required me to reach a settlement that was fair to both parties. As the months dragged on, our ability to reach an amicable solution seemed increasingly unlikely.

As the daughter of a successful entrepreneur, I was raised with business in my blood. In addition to my father's thriving medical practice, he also owns a car dealership, steak house, and drug screening/paternity testing firm in San Diego. I "learned the ropes" of each business from the ground floor and progressed through a series of management positions within the company. After receiving my degree in Business Administration in 2005 from the University of California at Davis, I became the Operations Manager for the entire firm.

In this capacity, I handle the accounting, marketing, advertising, customer service and human resource functions for each entity; I also serve as the plan administrator for the Southern California Maritime Consortium, which is a random drug testing program that is regulated by the US Navy. With the support of a great team, our businesses have earned a reputation for providing fast, honest and reliable service in the community.

Over the past several years, my job has required an increasing level of legal and financial expertise. As an orthopedic surgeon, my father treats many patients who have been injured in work-related accidents. As his corporate liaison, I coordinate patient files, speak to their attorneys and help to document their cases. I also manage all issues related to our insurance policies, zoning regulations, client confidentiality, tax liabilities and real estate. Increasingly, I am finding that my undergraduate training in business is not sufficient to handle these responsibilities with the appropriate care that they deserve.

My lack of financial expertise may ultimately hinder our corporate growth and direction. In 2009, an outside consultant drafted a comprehensive ten-year-plan to double our firm's growth. Without formal training is all aspects of business and the law, I am not qualified to execute the plan. I am eager to acquire a JD/MBA to guide my family's company throughout the challenges and pitfalls of the next century. Although my degrees will not give me an easy answer to every situation, I will be better prepared to make intelligent decisions that prevent future conflicts and protect the growth of our firm.

Fortunately, after months of negotiation, our attorney settled the Worker's Compensation claim with our waitress in a fair and equitable manner. I attribute the settlement largely to his patience, tenacity and seasoned negotiation skills. As I approach the JD/MBA admissions process, I am eager to develop my own strengths as the chief operating officer of my family's firm. My motivation is inherently personal, as our business represents the fruits of my father's labor and the dreams of our entire family. With their support, I am certain that I can handle the rigors of the dual degree program.

Our Assessment: In a short space, this candidate described her business expertise and her reasons for pursuing a JD/MBA. Her managerial background was an excellent fit for the program that accepted her.

Chapter 6: School-Specific Questions

Many law schools ask candidates to explain the factors that have shaped their identity – or how they will contribute to the diversity on campus. Other schools ask candidates to explain their fit for a particular program; out of all the options you have for your legal education, why did you pick *them*? If you encounter this question (or some variation of it), you must provide an answer that is focused, detailed, and persuasive, regardless of the length limit. Ideally, the information you present should complement – rather than duplicate – the material in your other essays for that school.

As always, the power is in the details. For the diversity question, you should tell your life story in a creative and entertaining way. Bear in mind, diversity encompasses far more than just your race; it also refers to your interests, talents, upbringing, religion, hobbies, family size, hometown, travel experiences, and socioeconomic standing. No two candidates have had the same life experiences, which is what makes this question interesting. If written honestly and openly, this essay can reveal a lot about who you are, what you value, and who you eventually hope to be.

The following essays vary widely in length and topic, but they all handled this type of question in an extraordinary way. By design, we have grouped the essays in the following sub-categories:

An Ethical Dilemma
Essays that Target a Specific School
How You Will Contribute to the School's Diversity

To protect the privacy of the writer, the names of all people, classes, schools, places, teams, activities, and companies have been changed.

An Ethical Dilemma

During my junior year at UCLA, I roomed with a friend I had known since grade school. At the beginning of our second semester, Justin began to exhibit erratic behavior. Every weekend, he drank excessively and did not return until the next morning. On several occasions, Justin bragged about his activities, which included the use of alcohol and illegal drugs. Not surprisingly, as his grades began to slip, Justin became increasingly withdrawn from his family and friends.

At first, I felt powerless to help him. Finally, after Justin was arrested for possession of cannabis, I refused to remain silent. With the support of two friends on the soccer team, I staged an intervention in our dorm room, where we confronted Justin about his self-destructive behavior. One by one, we expressed our concern for his welfare and our willingness to help him recover.

Unfortunately, Justin resented our efforts and refused to acknowledge his problem. In subsequent weeks, he continued to withdraw from us and to drink excessively. Eventually, he flunked out of UCLA and accepted a job at a fast food restaurant in our hometown. Our friendship, which had literally begun in the sandbox, was permanently damaged.

This experience gave me painful insight into the power of addiction. On a personal basis, it confirmed my decision to abstain from drinking and drugs. On a professional basis, it also demonstrated what I will eventually encounter by pursuing a career in criminal law. I am committed to saving lives by keeping drunk drivers off the street. Hopefully, by promoting compassionate sentencing laws, including mandatory counseling programs, I can help first-time offenders stop their self-destructive habits and live healther and more responsible lives.

<u>Our Assessment</u>: The ethical dilemma question is hard for most candidates, because they must choose a topic in which they honored their conscience and made the "correct" choice. Sometimes, those situations are too difficult or personal to talk about. Other times, the word limit is too short to really tell the story effectively. This author presented his dilemma in an effective way without exceeding the length limit. Although he and Justin did not enjoy a happy ending, the candidate made a genuine effort to help his friend turn his life around. The rest was beyond his control.

An Ethical Dilemma

At age six, I discovered that I was adopted. I also learned that I was a welcome gift to my loving parents, who had waited for several years to receive a healthy baby. Since then, I have always viewed adoption as a miraculous process that made the three of us a family.

In the same vein, I tend to have a negative view of abortion. At seventeen, I re-evaluated my perspective when my younger cousin unexpectedly became pregnant. To my surprise, she called me one evening and confided that she was thinking about having an abortion. My initial instinct was to tell her not to do it. However, I did not want to turn my cousin away when she desperately needed my acceptance and support.

During our conversation, I discovered the many factors that would influence her decision, including money, jobs, timing, and commitment. Although she loved her boyfriend, neither was prepared to raise and nurture a child. Finally, when I asked her about the possibility of adoption, my cousin quickly dismissed the idea. Once she saw the baby, she would never be able to give it away. My heart sank when I heard those words, because I knew that they were probably true.

In the end, I helped my cousin to evaluate the pros and cons of each option. When she asked my opinion, I told her that every choice had benefits and pitfalls. Although abortions are tragic, it is also tragic when children are abused by parents who are not ready or able to take care of them. Ultimately, she had to make the best decision on her own behalf, with no outside pressure.

This situation forced me to acknowledge my bias against abortion, which was stronger than I had imagined. Looking back, I am proud that I could set those feelings aside and offer unconditional support to my cousin. I also recognized that life presents everyone with situations that have no "easy" or obvious answers, because each alternative presents its own difficulties and tradeoffs. Rather than force my opinion on others, I will keep an open mind and allow them to make an informed choice that honors their individual needs. And, in return, I hope that they will offer me the same courtesy.

Our Assessment: This is a lovely essay on a highly controversial topic. The candidate handled it in a mature and loving way, without compromising her own feelings. She also provided unconditional support to her cousin during a difficult time, which was not the easiest thing to do. We have rarely seen this topic presented so honestly and objectively.

Targets a Specific School

After months of fruitless negotiation, the distraught single mother of five had abandoned all hope of resolving her problems with her landlord. Fortunately, a local legal clinic referred this case to my colleague at the Department of Justice, who agreed to represent the indigent client. After filing several motions and meeting with the opposing counsel, we settled the case and our client returned to her apartment.

While assisting attorneys at the Oakland Advice and Referral Clinic, I have gained considerable insight into the experiences of the poor and underprivileged in our society. As I learned how to assist clients who arrived at the legal intake center, I grew increasingly eager to assume the role of "lawyer" to champion their rights. More than any other professional, an attorney has the ability to break down barriers, assist those without a voice, and build a dialog between people from all walks of life. My long-term goal is to pursue a career in public interest law. Like the compassionate attorneys who do pro bono work, I hope to continue my advocacy through Columbia's Clinical Law Program and the Child Advocacy Law Clinic.

Columbia's enviable reputation in public interest law will help me to develop the goals and inspirations that define the best part of who I am. In addition, I look forward to obtaining a legal education at an institution that is strongly committed to internationalism. Columbia's requirement that all students complete a class in Transnational Law demonstrates its commitment to promoting social equality and justice on a global level. This philosophy will provide a nurturing environment for me to begin my legal career. My law degree, in addition to my background in economics and international relations, will provide the knowledge and credibility I need to achieve my professional goals.

Before I applied to Columbia, I spoke with several alumni to solicit their impressions of the program. Rhonda James, Lee Wang and Joel Pryce cited the strength of Columbia's mature student body and its insightful faculty and staff. They each found the coursework to be directly relevant to the problems they face in forming, leading and funding nonprofit organizations. As part of a multicultural student body, they gained an invaluable perspective of international law.

I left each discussion feeling invigorated and excited. After all, my expectations for my legal education are admittedly high. With my considerable professional experience, I want a program that is challenging and international in scope. I want to be surrounded by the best students, who will challenge me to exceed my comfort level and attain my highest potential. After considering the overwhelmingly positive feedback from several successful alumni, I am certain that Columbia will provide the skills I need to achieve my aggressive career goals.

Our Assessment: This candidate, who presented compelling recommendation letters to document her work as an advocate, tailored her essay to match the specific strengths that Columbia offers. She also arranged for the alumni she mentioned in the letter to write letters of support on her behalf. In the end, this focused approach was highly successful for her.

Targets a Specific School

My position as a fiction editor at Harper Collins has confirmed my suitability for a career in publishing. I love everything about the job, from reading unpolished manuscripts to coordinating whirlwind promotional tours in exotic places like Sproul, Iowa. Over the past five years, I have edited three blockbuster diet books, including *Thighbusters* by Zora Delany, which spent an unprecedented seventy-nine weeks at the top of the *New York Times* Bestseller List. As I become increasingly comfortable with selecting and editing content, I yearn to explore the legal aspects of the industry.

When I read a promising manuscript, I know that several other publishing houses are probably also interested in the book. Our success in wooing the author will invariably hinge on drafting the most attractive contract, which will define their initial advance, profit percentage, promotional and licensing fees and television and media rights to the material. Our failure to land a potential bestseller is rarely our inability to see the work's potential, but a reflection of a failed or inefficient negotiation.

After three promotions as an editor, I am eager to embrace the legal, rather than creative, challenges in the publishing industry. To move into this type of position, I need to learn how to negotiate the firm's arrangements with authors, agents and vendors. I need a better appreciation of the growth potential of the industry, considering the increasing competition from internet re-sellers, such as Amazon and Half.com. Even "novelty" items, like e-books, will affect the way that a traditional publishing house does business in the next century.

Steeped in tradition, the publishing industry resists change, yet the rapid developments in media technology present unprecedented challenges for which we must ultimately be prepared. As new channels of distribution, including electronic and online services, gain market share from bricks-and-mortar bookstores, existing publishing houses must be ready to counter with their own original sales and marketing techniques. We must remain ahead of the technology curve and be prepared to deliver better, faster and more reliable products in a global economy. As I am typing this, no one knows what those products will be. Indeed, the very notion of what a publisher does will continue to evolve in the next few years. I want to be prepared to handle the complex legal challenges that this transition will present.

When I decided to obtain my law degree, I never considered any school except Columbia. Our senior counsel, Carla Stephens, and her associate, Claude White, are both 1979 graduates of your program. Over the years, I have heard nothing but praise for your progressive faculty, who provide a healthy balance of classroom and real-world experience. I also cannot imagine a better place to live than New York City, which is the heart of the publishing industry. During a 2008 summer course in Business Law at Columbia, Professor John Vernon seriously encouraged me to apply. Although I am not your typical candidate, he thought I would bring a novel perspective to your program. After all, in a sea of future prosecutors, someone has to have a creative flair!

Our Assessment: This author is a successful publishing executive who transitioned her career to the legal side of the field. This essay eloquently expresses her passion for the field and her reasons for selecting Columbia.

Targets a Specific School

Georgetown University School of Law offers a rare educational dichotomy; as one of the oldest and most distinguished programs in the United States, its environment is steeped in history and tradition, yet it retains sufficient flexibility to meet the changing needs of the legal community. Since opening its doors in 1790, Georgetown has set the standard for excellence in numerous aspects of legal education. onsequently, I am eager to explore its many academic, clinical and extracurricular opportunities.

With my background in business and international law, I am eager to take interdisciplinary classes in these areas at Georgetown. By completing elective courses at the business school, I can augment my law degree with a Certificate of Study in Business Policy and Management. Additionally, Georgetown offers numerous courses in international and comparative law that are taught by renowned experts in the field. I am particularly impressed by the accessibility of the faculty members, who eat lunch with first-year students. By establishing close relationships between the students and professors, Georgetown will enhance my educational experience and help me to become a better litigator.

As a prospective student, I am most impressed by Georgetown's commitment to the clinical aspects of legal education. Georgetown was the first major law school to develop a clinical program, which continues to hold an enviable reputation in the academic community. The benefits of the program are immeasurable, both to the students and to the clients they serve. By working on actual cases under the supervision of an attorney, I can put my classroom knowledge into action on a client's behalf. In recent years, students at the clinic have tried civil cases in Philadelphia and worked for US Senators in Washington, DC. By the time they graduate, they know their way around a courtroom and are better prepared to handle the daily challenges of the profession.

As a advocate for numerous social and political issues, I am delighted to know that Georgetown shares my commitment to providing pro bono services in disadvantaged communities. Through my previous volunteer efforts in Ghana, India the United States, I have seen the powerful changes that an advocate can accomplish and I am eager to lend my skills to similar efforts at Georgetown. With my background in business and entrepreneurship, I am a great fit for the Pro Bono Business Clinic, which provides hands-on experience and free legal counsel to fledgling businesses. By helping entrepreneurs bring their professional dreams to fruition, I will learn from their experiences and further develop my skills.

On a personal level, Georgetown also offers meaningful extracurricular activities that will broaden my social network. As an undergraduate student, I used my platform as the editor of a campus newspaper to promote the spirit of diversity on campus. I am eager to participate in the Asian-American Legal Studies Association at Georgetown, which shares a similar goal. I also hope to contribute to *The Georgetown University Law Review,* which is one of the oldest and most well known publications in the profession.

During my recent visit to Georgetown, I marveled at the school's ability to preserve its beautiful architecture and sense of history, while providing a progressive environment to meet its students' needs. Georgetown's campus in Washington, DC offers the close-knit atmosphere of a small town within a large cosmopolitan city. After living in San Francisco for several years, I appreciate the dual benefits of this unique environment, including the opportunity to network with faculty and alumni in the DC area.

After evaluating the merits of several law schools, I cannot imagine a better place for me than Georgetown. I am eager to uphold the school's tradition of excellence, which continually raises the level of performance and expectations of its faculty and students. If admitted, I will leave my own lasting imprint on Georgetown's rich and vibrant culture.

<u>Our Assessment</u>: Although long, this essay gives the reader an excellent feel for the many strengths the candidate will bring to Georgetown. She also took the time to research the school and confirm her fit for their program, which was much appreciated.

Targets a Specific School

For several compelling reasons, Columbia is my first choice for my legal education. First, Columbia has taken the initiative to recruit outstanding law professors with decades of expertise in intellectual property law. With full-time professors such as Dr. Jack Myers and Dr. Carole Wong, who argued the defendant's case in *Collins vs. Davis,* I will learn the nuances of the law from the seasoned professionals who litigated landmark cases. Second, I am eager to contribute to the efforts of the Columbia Public Interest Law Center, which provides pro-bono legal services to indigent clients in New York City. The program is similar in mission and scope to Helping Hands, where I have volunteered for the past three years.

Third, finding like-minded classmates in law school will make the demanding experience richer, friendlier and more fruitful. My perspective is not that of a young idealist, but of a Ph.D. who has completed three academic degrees at small liberal arts colleges. Although the schools I attended attracted bright, exceptional students, I often had to search off-campus for expertise in my area. Columbia's size, breadth of course offerings and commitment to quality suggest that it will be a highly demanding educational experience. Further, the stringent admissions criteria suggest that my law school peers will share my commitment to academic rigor.

Fourth, Columbia's reputation for supporting candidates who are committed to intellectual property law ensures that the class will contain a high percentage of students who are dedicated to such work. As the holder of three US Patents in the biotechnology area, I have a strong interest in pursuing a career as a patent attorney. Columbia's reputation in this area is unparalleled, both for its faculty expertise and the availability of internships. I am particularly intrigued by the possibility of working in the US Patent Office as part of my three-year program.

Fifth, because I will arrive at law school with a successful background as an entrepreneur and a keen interest in business law, I cannot overstate the appeal of having access to Columbia's nationally recognized business faculty. I am excited by the prospect of enrolling in international business classes with Professor Richard Clark, whose research in technology law played a key role in defining the scope of my Ph.D. project.

Sixth, as a native of New York City, the opportunity to study law in my hometown is quite appealing. In addition to being able to live with my family, I will enjoy the benefits of internships at many of the city's finer law firms. Since I hope to pass the bar in New York, I am eager to begin my professional networking while I attend law school.

Finally, after graduation, my dream has always been to work as an attorney in the US Patent Office. My research suggests that Columbia graduates compete well for such highly competitive jobs. In a discussion with faculty member Dr. Nathan Unger, he confirmed that Columbia graduates are highly coveted because of their exceptional training in intellectual property law. Therefore, I cannot imagine a better place for me than Columbia.

Our Assessment: The author of this statement is a seasoned entrepreneur with a distinguished track record in his field. In this essay, he clearly and succinctly states his reasons for choosing Columbia, which is perfectly aligned with his interests and goals. The logical way that he listed his points (first, second, third, etc.) was simply part of his personality.

Targets a Specific School

As I prepare for a career in financial law, the JD/MBA program at the University of Chicago is an ideal place for me. The school's location on the Magnificent Mile offers a unique perspective of the challenges and opportunities in the volatile commodities market. During my campus tour, I noted its close proximity to the Chicago Board of Trade, along with numerous government centers and cultural hubs in the center of the city. The Metro stop on campus makes this entire world easily accessible. I was also impressed by the vibrant international feel of the campus and surrounding metropolitan area, where global decisions are made each day. What better place to begin my career?

As one of the few top universities to offer a dual JD/MBA program, Chicago acknowledges the need to provide comprehensive training to candidates with career aspirations in financial law. The benefits to the students are immeasurable. While I pursue my coursework in torts and contracts, I can compete for an internship at the IMF or Chicago Board of Trade. Upon graduation, I will be conversant in all aspects of financial management and forensic accounting, and will be qualified to investigate cases of investor fraud, improper accounting and SEC violations. Exposure to a government agency at this stage of my life will provide a solid foundation for my eventual career.

My final motivating factor to attend the University of Chicago is its unparalleled reputation in the academic, business and political communities. Several of my colleagues at JP Morgan Chase are Chicago alumni, who have cited their satisfaction with their classes, professors, internships and campus life. During my visit to the school, I was impressed by the first-class facilities and demonstrated commitment to graduate teaching. I am also excited about the opportunity to pursue relevant volunteer activities on the Chicago campus.

For several years, I have worked as an advisor to the Lexington chapter of Entrepreneurial Kids, a non-profit agency that locates funding for student businesses. I have also enjoyed considerable success mentoring high school students who are eager to pursue an entrepreneurial path. While in Chicago, I will lend my support to the local chapter of Fast Start, which has an excellent reputation for its community education program for the self-employed. Through the local Big Brothers program, I can also continue my volunteer work as a mentor for teenage boys with special needs. Chicago offers an unparalleled opportunity for me to work in these areas and share my expertise with a new generation of talented kids.

After I graduate, Chicago's business and legal community will offer intriguing challenges for my skills in business law. With its large concentration of publicly-held companies, the area struggles to attract and retain qualified candidates who specialize in forensic accounting. Following graduation, I hope to work in this area, where I will assist with SEC investigations. Armed with an exceptional education from Chicago, I will be well prepared to keep abreast of the rapidly-evolving technology that is used to solve white collar crimes. I am eager to take my place in this vibrant intellectual community.

Our Assessment: This candidate cited numerous ways that the JD/MBA program at Chicago would allow him to learn, grow, and contribute. He also included relevant details from his campus visit, which personalized the essay and made it memorable. The statement was well perceived.

Diversity

Every day, after the final bell at school, I ran to the convenience store in downtown Cicero that my parents owned and operated. Between four and midnight, I served a steady stream of customers who bought gas, snack food, and lottery tickets on their way home from work. To my younger siblings, this was a thankless job with few intrinsic rewards. Yet, to me, our successful business was proof of our family's ability to build a successful life in America. By working hard and watching our finances, my parents managed to purchase a home, launch their business, and support our large extended family in India. As a result, I was convinced that I would enjoy a comparable level of success by following their example.

Unfortunately, due to the demands of the store, my parents viewed my work there as a higher priority than my education. Consequently, I often skipped classes and worked late into the night when my father was short-handed. Everything changed in 2009, when he collapsed at the store and died from a heart attack. In subsequent days, we learned that the trappings of success that we had enjoyed were all an illusion; beyond the assets in the store, there was no money or life insurance to pay our ongoing expenses. Instead, we were forced to close the store and sell the inventory for pennies on the dollar. A year later, we moved into a homeless shelter when the bank foreclosed on the home that my parents had worked so hard to buy.

This life-changing event taught me a powerful lesson in humility. In an instant, we went from successful entrepreneurs to grieving survivors who relied upon public assistance. Although I was grateful for the help that we received, I was determined to acquire the education I would need to support my family and serve as an example for others. Balancing a job with the demands of my classes presented formidable time and logistical challenges. Nevertheless, I was determined to set a positive example for my siblings by handling them with grace and dignity.

I also discovered that my family's problems were far from unique. In our minority neighborhood, formal education is rarely a priority. As a result, few children have the academic training and practical experience they need to make wise decisions about their future. Like many children from immigrant families, I struggled to succeed in an educational system with which my parents were not familiar. Fortunately, I had a strong support system in Cicero's Indian-American community, which kept me focused on my long-term goals.

Next month, I will proudly graduate from Syracuse University with a perfect GPA. I have also received scholarship awards from the YWCA, the Elk Society, and the Middle Eastern Academic Symposium. I would never have received these honors without the support of my family, friends, teachers, and mentors, who had tremendous faith in my ability to create a better future. They also ignited my desire to share the benefits of my education with those who have not enjoyed similar opportunities.

Far too often, the kids in my neighborhood are forced to drop out of school in order to support their families. Without the benefits of a college degree, they cannot obtain a good job or build a successful life. As someone who was fortunate enough to escape a dead-end existence, I am determined to pave a clear path for others to do the same.

Today, because of my support system, I have escaped the temptations of drugs and violence that plague the streets of Cicero. Most importantly, I have realized that education is the only path to a safe and successful future, in which there truly are no limits. After law school, I hope to launch a non-profit organization that serves the needs of inner city children. By doing so, I can find practical ways to transform communities through the power of a positive example. At the very least, I can encourage other children to stay in school and fulfill their academic potential.

Our Assessment: This candidate faced formidable obstacles to graduate from college, support his family, and build a successful life. By positioning himself as a survivor (rather than a victim), he gained considerable respect from the committee, who knew that he had the strength and tenacity to help others succeed.

Diversity

Last fall, I participated in a humanitarian mission trip that literally transformed my life. I accompanied five members of the International Red Cross team to Darfur, where we assisted civilians who were displaced by the war between the government and the indigenous population. Upon my arrival, I witnessed the ongoing threats that the residents endure, including poverty, disease, malnutrition, and random violence. On my first day, a military official showed us how to identify, extract, and de-activate a landmine. He also explained how to protect ourselves if we encountered an armed terrorist. These experiences showed me the daily reality of the locals, who were trapped in a violent world in which the danger was impossible to predict.

The following day, we distributed dry rations, new clothes, and school supplies at an orphanage that housed more than 100 survivors of the recent violence. A number of the children had lost not only their homes, but their entire family. It was humbling to know that the supplies we delivered, including vitamins, antibiotics, and bandages, could be used to save a life.

Throughout our trip, we spent considerable time traveling among the various facilities that needed our help. After our trip to the orphanage, we visited a makeshift Red Cross Hospital in Darfur, which had been destroyed by several terrorist attacks. Along the way, we stopped at camps that provided temporary shelter for people who were displaced by the civil war. According to our team leader, who had visited the same camps a year before, hundreds of occupants had already found permanent rehabilitation. However, we also spoke to several people who were still waiting for a safe place to live, and were forced to stay in overcrowded camps that lack clean water, healthy food, sanitary conditions, and security. Not surprisingly, in this unhealthy and impoverished environment, few people have hope for a safe future.

In our free time, we helped our host family with their small farming business, which bore little resemblance to the industrial facilities in developed nations. With no money, machinery, or fertilizer, the farmers in Darfur rely upon rain, hard work, and the power of their cattle to plough the soil. Their yield, of course, is dependent upon the amount of rainfall the area receives; during times of drought, the farmers barely make enough money to survive. As I watched them work, I was amazed by their ability to move quickly and easily through the thick mud. The volunteers, in contrast, struggled to take a single step in these intense conditions. When I removed my boots at the end of the day, I had a newfound appreciation for the labor required to harvest a single serving of food.

On my long ride home, I realized how blessed I am to live in a safe home with a loving family that has the physical, financial, and emotional support to face life's challenges. In contrast, the people in Darfur, though no fault of their own, struggle arduously simply to survive. By volunteering for the International Red Cross, I fulfilled my desire to visit a part of my continent that had been completely alien to me. As summer begins, I am eager to visit the region again, to continue the work for such a noble cause. Surely, during my years at Columbia, I can convince my fellow students to support similar humanitarian initiatives, which serve the needs of deserving residents of the war-torn regions of Africa.

Our Assessment: This essay revealed the candidate's observations of a war-torn area, where the residents struggle simply to survive. His commitment to helping them, which is confirmed in the final paragraph of his essay, confirms that this trip made a lasting impact on his life.

Diversity

Popular clichés about "appearances being deceiving" are particularly true for to those of multi-cultural heritage. By appearance, I am a stereotypical Asian woman with dark hair, olive skin and brown eyes. Yet my life in Spain and the United States has been decidedly "Western," which has provided a powerful contrast to my upbringing in China. I have spent nearly thirty years bridging the gap between three very different cultures and carving out an identity that is uniquely my own.

My resume presents a powerful contrast between my professional image and the personal strengths that I will bring to my law school class. On one hand, I am a highly trained engineer who solves problems using my technical skills and analytical mind. On the other hand, I am also a risk taker who is not afraid to embrace challenges and discover my talents in different areas. My classmates will undoubtedly discover that I am open to new possibilities and supportive of the dreams of others.

My risk taking began at age sixteen, when I moved to Spain to attend high school. I will never forget my mother's tears when I left her at the airport in China. At the time, I didn't realize the significance of the moment or how my world was about to change. Life soon presented me with an additional and unexpected challenge; my aunt passed away after my arrival in Spain, which left me self-supporting at age sixteen. Despite this setback, I refused to abandon my dream of obtaining an education. I worked two jobs to pay my way through high school. As one of only three engineering scholarship holders in Spain, I went on to receive my degree in electronic engineering.

My passion for risk taking inspired me to set (and achieve) a number of personal and professional goals. In college, I opted to study Japanese, which was one of the most difficult language courses. With the recommendation of my Japanese tutor, I was accepted to a summer program in advanced Japanese language and culture at Tokyo's International University. Although challenging, the risk paid off. My fluency in Japanese has broadened my understanding of Asian cultures and helped me to develop friendships that would not otherwise be possible.

My riskiest personal venture was overcoming my fear of heights. For many years, this phobia restricted what I was willing to do. Simple things, like stepping into an elevator, would cause my knees to knock. As a student engineer, I attended a training course in Spain's Lake District, which required me to climb a 100-foot hill and swing down the other side by holding onto a single rope. Even with the help of an instructor, my fear was palpable. I watched with empathy as several other female students gave up. Yet when my own turn came, I refused to succumb to my fear.

The initial climb was easy, as my small hands gingerly grabbed the edge of each rock. Then, I made the fatal mistake of looking down at my teammates, which revealed how high I was. In a split second, all of the old feelings came rushing back. My stomach turned and my knees became weak. I wondered how I would take my next breath. As my mind raced with fear, I heard my teammates cheering me on from their respective places on the hill. With their support, I knew that I could continue. I felt an indescribable joy when the instructor helped me on the last few steps. I had, once again, exceeded my own expectations and achieved the impossible. My climbing experience reinforced the importance of facing my fears and taking calculated risks.

Throughout my life, my most fulfilling experiences have required me to open my mind to new people, places and challenges. By enrolling in law school, I will embrace the opportunity to augment my skills in technology with expertise in international law. I am certain the experience will open the door to a new and exciting future.

Our Assessment: This essay, although long, gives keen insight into the challenges the candidate faced to complete her education and build a successful life. The additional material about her fear of heights was particularly valuable, because it made the essay (and candidate) memorable; it also cemented her reputation as a risk taker.

Diversity

Looking back, I blame "family drive." There I was, in the middle of my winter break, driving to our nation's capital. As I passed each mile marker, my lifelong dream was quickly becoming a reality. Nevertheless, for a brief spell in Kentucky, I was filled with anxiety and apprehension. In a few short hours, I would exchange my comfortable identity as a college student for that of a D.C. Intern.

For someone who was raised in a large city, moving to Washington D.C. may not seem like a big deal. Yet, for a country boy from Burns, Wyoming (population 2,000), living in D.C. was a daunting proposition. Throughout my childhood, I formed life-long friendships and gained invaluable respect for the people in my small hometown. In a community as tight-knit as Burns, "love thy neighbor" is a lifestyle that we take quite seriously.

So is hard work. At fourteen, I began to work in my family's pizza restaurant, where I bussed tables and waited on customers. While most teens spent Friday and Saturday nights with their friends, I was happy to clean the ovens. Not only was I a vital cog in my family's business; I also developed organizational and communication skills from my long hours of work. At a young age, I took great pride in serving a good product in a clean environment with exceptional service.

Defying the laid back mid western stereotype, my family possessed a strong motivation for success. As the youngest child, I watched my father work countless hours during the week preparing tax returns for his clients. I also observed my three older siblings pursue higher education and successful business ventures. My childhood was guided by two unspoken assumptions: (1) hard work leads to success, and (2) failure is not an option. Thanks to my parents' nurturing, I share this "family drive," which empowers me to achieve my dreams.

Thanks to my support network in Burns, I had the confidence to accept an internship clear across the country, where I didn't know a soul. As I stood outside the door to U.S. Term Limits (my new employer), I was ready for the challenges of D.C. politics. My life changed instantaneously. As I heard so often from the Washington D.C. citizenry, "I wasn't in Wyoming anymore." My job at U.S. Term Limits was fast-paced, multifaceted and fun. On any given day, I would give a speech, talk to a Senator or draft a report for voters. By assuming substantial responsibilities for voter education, I ultimately learned invaluable research techniques. I also flexed my organizational skills. After a legislative victory, I took charge of a press conference, reserved a conference room and made travel arrangements for legislators from California. I was completely energized by my involvement in the successful event.

When I drove back to Wyoming at the end of my internship, I was filled with mixed emotions. I was eager to see my family and friends, yet I was sorry to leave the life I had built in our nation's capitol. My internship confirmed many of life's unspoken lessons about hard work and taking risks. By leaving the Wyoming plains, I confirmed my interest in a legal career, which offers myriad opportunities to use my skills to promote voter awareness and education.

As I pulled into my driveway in Burns, I knew that I would take the chance to apply to law school. Throughout my life, I have embraced diverse opportunities to learn, grow and discover my strengths. I am eager to begin the next part of my journey, whether it takes me to skyline of New York City or to the beaches of Miami. Once again, I blame my unflagging confidence on "family drive."

Our Assessment: This essay, although long, tells the candidate's story in a relaxed, conversational style. After reading it, the committee felt like they knew him, which was the first step to saying "yes."

Diversity

Imagine having to put together a jigsaw puzzle with only half the pieces given to you. Through a series of scavenger hunts, you must find or create the remaining pieces to complete the final picture. Some would call this a profound challenge, while others would call it an exercise in futility. I call it life.

As an Iranian male, I was raised with a powerful sense of "Izaat," or respect, for my family's culture. My father taught me from an early age that respect was more important than wealth, happiness and even health. Throughout my childhood, my choices (or puzzle pieces) were selected by my parents in accordance to their cherished cultural values. The first puzzle piece I selected for myself was a college education, rather than working in my family's electronics business. Unlike my older brother, who was predestined by family legacy to become a physician, I had my family's blessing to choose my own destiny. What a marvelous gift! By choosing education, my brother and I became the first members of our tribal community to obtain college degrees. Ultimately, we embraced a challenging path that was very different from anything our parents had ever experienced.

In college, I balanced my academic curriculum with my participation in intercollegiate football, student senate and volunteer activities. These experiences taught me that I could achieve highly aggressive goals via dedication and commitment. Many nights, Coach Myers made us run goal-posts until our faces turned purple and we silently questioned why we were doing it. Between each gaser, the Coach would always say "mental toughness" and "extreme desire." A year or so later, I realized that these two cornerstone principles led our team to the division championship. Even now, they are the principles that continue to govern my life.

In choosing my profession, I naturally gravitated to business. By nature, I think logically, question the status quo and refuse to accept limitations. I began my career as an assistant to Robert Levin, the owner of QVC's Home Shopping Network. During my first several months with the firm, I worked tirelessly on a project to promote Susan Lucci's line of costume jewelry. After several months of creative cross promotions, Susan's line enjoyed the highest sales in QVC history. Since graduating from Yale University in 2006, I have worked as a promotions manager for QVC; in this capacity, I handle all television and radio advertising in the United States and Canada. I am also investigating opportunities to promote the company's thirty-four product lines on the Internet.

My long-term dream is to be the president of an international firm such as QVC, which markets designer items online. At this point in my career, this may seem like an elusive fantasy. An Iranian Muslim, a naturalized citizen, striving to become a CEO of a thriving global enterprise? Nevertheless, I am passionate about achieving my goal. In my heart, I know that my calling is to infuse the business and legal communities with a much-needed sense of diversity. My father has always told me that for every obstacle there are hundreds (if not thousands) of opportunities. With my heartfelt dedication, I will embrace every chance to achieve my dreams.

Each unique life experience has provided another piece of the puzzle and prepared me for the challenges of a legal career. By setting and achieving aggressive goals, I have proven to myself that I have the drive, faith and passion I will need to become a successful attorney and CEO. I am eager to embrace my legal education as the next piece of my life's puzzle, which will prepare me for a lifetime of continual success.

Our Assessment: This candidate presented his life's journey as a puzzle that he had to solve by finding and assembling the correct pieces. Thanks to the strength of his material and the creative way that he presented it, the essay was well perceived.

Diversity

When I returned to South Dakota after graduating from Princeton University, I struggled with the culture shock of moving from a diverse and tolerant community to one that seemed to lack both qualities. As I mourned the loss of the social camaraderie that I had enjoyed for four years, I discovered Women for America, a political advocacy group with a local chapter in Pierre. After reading the group's objectives, I suddenly felt a renewed sense of purpose; here was an environment in which I could discuss social issues and assume my rightful place as an advocate for women's rights.

After attending my first meeting, I began to take action: I contacted my senators and representatives about my concerns regarding women's health care; I wrote letters to the editor to explain that one could be both a feminist and pro-family; and I began conversing with co-workers and strangers about their political views about federally-funded abortions. Depending on whether our cumulative actions seemed to be making a difference, I alternated between feeling encouraged and defeated. Then, when I least expected, I received a rare opportunity to share my voice. Through Women for America, I was invited to meet with my state senator, who wanted to hear the thoughts of a "young, highly educated woman" on a variety of political issues. I never expected that this simple meeting would so elucidate my understanding of democracy.

At first, I gave little thought to my scheduled meeting with South Dakota's Democratic Senator Tom Daschle. Eventually, though, I became intimidated by the dozens of suggestions and proposed questions for him that I received via email. As I tried to memorize the relevant statistics on six or seven issues, I questioned whether I should back out of the meeting. After all, what could I, a 23-year-old with little practical experience, add to the discussion? With limited seats at the meeting, I hoped that I was qualified enough to justify taking one.

Upon my arrival, I was immediately disarmed by Senator Daschle's grace and humor. After an illustrious political career, he was completely at ease making the requisite small talk that the occasion required. By the time we sat down with the Senator's press secretary and deputy director, I had already come to feel a sense of camaraderie with the group. At our small round table, the Senator and his aides were not millionaires, public figures or publicity-seeking celebrities; they were simply American citizens who were trying to put the ideals of democracy into action.

Looking back, the meeting was an amazing opportunity for learning and growth. We took turns telling our personal stories and giving a voice to our shared concerns. We were Democrats and Republicans. We were women and men. We were single, married, old, young, rich and poor. And yet, the twelve of us shared one vision and one simple expectation: that the Senator know that his constituents cared about women's rights in the United States and were committed to equality in all aspects of society. Regardless of his own personal and religious biases, we expected him to act with integrity on issues that were important to us. I left the meeting feeling more empowered than I had in years.

To an outsider, attending the meeting may seem like a trivial act. After all, I only did what thousands of Americans do every day; I contacted my legislator and agreed to meet with him. And yet, my experience that day proved incredibly powerful in shaping my vision of what it means to be an American. As I prepare to embark on a legal career, I am simultaneously grateful and humbled to live in the wealthiest nation in the world. Through my work with Women for America, I am aware of the pressing need for attorneys and legislators who will lobby for improved access to health care for poor women and children. Thanks to my meeting with Senator Daschle, I know that fulfilling this need is not only my calling, but my personal responsibility.

Our Assessment: This essay, which focused on a single theme, was powerful due to the candidate's enthusiasm and easy writing style. Her story about meeting the Senator dovetailed nicely with her primary statement, which discussed her volunteer work in the health care arena.

Diversity

As a first-generation Chinese-American, I will add a unique voice to the academic and cultural richness of XXXXX Law School. Since arriving in the United States at age eight, I have continued to explore several aspects of my Chinese heritage. I speak fluent Mandarin and am an avid fan of Huangmeixi, which is a style of Chinese Opera that is unfamiliar to most of my Asian friends. Furthermore, despite being raised in the US, I tend to embody my parents' conservative perspective on academic and social matters. As part of the first generation to enroll in college after the Chinese Cultural Revolution, my parents have always stressed the importance of acquiring a solid technical education. With their support, I decided to complete my undergraduate degree in engineering, which gave me the discipline and analytical skills to succeed in the legal profession.

Although I am proud of my heritage, I have never forgotten my status as a "minority" in the highly diverse American society. During my middle school and high school years, I was one of the few non-Caucasians in an otherwise homogeneous environment. Although most of my peers were open-minded and tolerant, a few students harassed me with childish racial taunts. I fought back against this discrimination with the support of my teachers and school administrators.

This first-hand experience with intolerance taught me the importance of maintaining a diverse social network, which was critical at Stanford, where Asians are one of the majority cultures. Although I was tempted to join all-Asian cliques during my undergraduate years, I refused to limit the types of people that I would befriend. Instead, I expanded my comfort zone by joining several martial arts clubs, which provided a surprisingly diverse social network. My decision had unexpected personal benefits. By getting to know very different types of people, I have become more socially mature and more appreciative of the "American" aspects of my personality. This cooperative spirit will be an asset in law school and in my eventual legal career, when I will work with people from all nations and all walks of life.

Our Assessment: This is a "traditional" diversity essay, which focuses on the candidate's efforts to combine both halves of his cultural heritage. Although shorter and less stylish than the other examples in this book, it is an effective essay that reveals considerable details about the candidate's background, interests, and skills that were not included in his primary statement.

Diversity – Discrimination in a Foreign Country

After completing my degree in International Relations at the University of Wyoming, I lived for three years in a small village on the outskirts of Kyoto, Japan, where I was the only blond, blue-eyed man most people had ever seen. Although I always felt conspicuous, as a senior engineer at an international electronics company,

I did not expect to be an object of discrimination….and yet I was. My personal encounters with prejudice and injustice in Japan have inspired my work as an advocate for change.

During a ski trip to Nagano with three Japanese friends, I encountered a hotel with a "Japanese Only" sign posted at the door. Although my friends complained about the policy, the owner was intransigent. I was not allowed to stay there. A year later, I had a similar experience when I went apartment hunting. Before I could greet the real estate agent, he pushed me back to the door shouting (In Japanese) "No way." When I asked him why, he added "No foreigners!" Although I found an agent who was willing to work with me, I encountered similar attitudes from other close-minded landlords. They cited a litany of ridiculous reasons for not renting to me, because foreigners "cook strange food, can't speak Japanese, and would not understand the customs."

Unwilling to accept such shabby treatment, I scoured the internet for other like-minded Japanese who thought this type of behavior was reprehensible. Then, I contacted an American in Sapporo who had filed the first lawsuit in Japan to challenge the "Japanese Only" signs. He inspired me to join a human rights group called Equality Now, which promotes multicultural understanding by fighting discrimination and unjust laws. As our membership grows, we continue to disseminate information and lobby the government to champion individual rights. Nevertheless, change comes slowly in Japan and for different reasons than in America. To my dismay, even business owners who believe the "Japanese Only" policy is legally and morally unjust refuse to take down the signs. In Japan, individual rights are less important than retaining loyal customers and group harmony.

Since joining Equality Now, I have read everything I could find about Japanese law, including the constitution. Although I will not change the system single-handedly, I am proud to promote an important cause that permeates all cultures and societies. As Robert Kennedy eloquently stated, "Each time a man stands up for an ideal, or acts to improve the lot of others, or strikes out against injustice, he sends forth a tiny ripple of hope, and crossing each other from a million different centers of energy of daring, those ripples build a current that can sweep down the mightiest walls of oppression and resistance." I can't imagine a more fulfilling future than fighting injustice in whatever guise it may appear.

Our Assessment: This is an excellent diversity essay from someone who experienced discrimination in another country and channeled his anger and frustration into meaningful volunteer work. As part of his application, the candidate submitted a recommendation letter from the president of Equality Now, who cited his contribution to their work. The essay and letter were well perceived.

Chapter 7: Addendums to Explain Unusual Situations

Ideally, in a perfect world, your grades and test scores will be an excellent fit for the law school that you hope to attend. But what if they aren't? Many times, as part of their applications, candidates will attach a separate addendum to explain a disappointing grade or LSAT score. Their hope is that the explanation will compensate for a less than stellar "number" on their application. From our experience, these addendums rarely make a positive impact on the admissions committee.

Why? Most explanations are highly personal and difficult to verify. Other times, the excuse raises more questions than it actually answers, such as an announcement that the candidate does not perform well on standardized tests. Well, top law schools *require* candidates to pass dozens of timed tests in a highly competitive environment. If you cannot handle the LSAT, which is the only "constant" in the application process, how do you plan to compete in the classroom....or pass your bar exam, which is the ultimate timed test? (I've yet to hear a persuasive answer to that question.)

Nevertheless, if you have a disappointing grade or LSAT score – and a legitimate explanation for it – you should definitely explain the situation to the admissions committee in the form of a short, well-written addendum. If possible, you should also have an objective third party (who has no vested interest in the admissions decision) document the situation in a persuasive recommendation letter.

What are legitimate explanations?

- Medical emergencies that can be documented by a physician's letter
- A serious illness or death in the immediate family
- Military commitments/relocations
- Work commitments necessitated by financial emergencies
- Your native language is not English
- You have a documented learning disability, but did not request special accommodations for the LSAT

In these cases, a well-written addendum that informs the committee of the situation (without making excuses) can greatly enhance your application. At the very least, it will give the reader some insight into the problems you have faced to complete your education and pursue your professional goals. This chapter contains several addendums that candidates submitted to explain a disappointing GPA or LSAT score. We have also included addendums to explain other troublesome blemishes, such as an arrest record, job loss, or gap in employment history.

To protect the privacy of the applicant, the names of all people, classes, schools, places, and companies have been changed.

Addendum to Explain Bad Grades

Although my recent academic performance is excellent, I wasn't always able to devote my complete energy to my school work. I was enrolled in the American International University during the collapse of the Colombian government, when the country underwent unprecedented economic turmoil and uncertainty. In a short period of time, my country experienced hyperinflation, rampant unemployment and a dramatic increase in violent crime. My family and I lost our life savings, including our family business. As a result, I found myself struggling to survive, rather than focusing on school.

Looking back, I am proud that I was able to balance my schoolwork with a full-time job at a restaurant. I did everything possible to ensure my family's survival during an extremely difficult time. Yet the stress of the economic overhaul made it impossible for me to concentrate on my studies. Many days, rather than prepare for exams, I stood in long lines to buy food. Thus, my grades from the American International University reflect the stress of these dire circumstances, rather than my actual ability.

Fortunately, they also show that I am a survivor. During a tumultuous situation, I was forced to re-evaluate my beliefs, aspirations and plans – and I simply refused to give up. Although my grades suffered, the experience clarified my goals, challenged my organizational skills and provided the strength I needed to overcome formidable obstacles. I am a survivor. What better strengths to bring to a legal career?

Our Assessment: This essay is short, focused, and sincere; it also contains information that can easily be verified by third-party sources. For one of his recommendations, this candidate submitted a letter from a professor in Colombia, who cited his extraordinary performance under pressure. The committee realized that he was an intelligent and hardworking young man who had done his best under difficult circumstances.

Addendum to Explain Bad Grades

When evaluating my application, I hope the committee will take into consideration my difficult adjustment to the United States. I moved to San Francisco at age fifteen, not knowing a word of English. My salvation was the school's bilingual education program, where I learned how to speak and write English, in addition to perfecting my fluency in Mandarin. With the tireless support of the faculty, I plunged into my new life in America, determined to embrace the many opportunities that were unavailable in my native Beijing.

Unfortunately, the language barrier prevented me from competing successfully with other students who were native speakers of English. Although I worked incredibly hard, my grades were primarily Bs and Cs, rather than the As I desired. Fortunately, as my English improved, so did my grades. By senior year, I was in the top 10% of my class, and won first place in the Westinghouse science competition. I was also elected as captain of Barrington High School's nationally acclaimed debate team.

Throughout my life, I have become deeply appreciative of the opportunities I have reaped by living in America. Yet my struggle to perfect the English language is most certainly reflected in my grades. With this in mind, I hope the committee will consider the tremendous challenges that my relocation required. In addition to learning a new language, I also had to adjust to a new culture and carve out a unique set of values and goals. This maturity will make me a more competent and empathetic attorney.

Compared to other programs, XXX Law School offers a solid academic reputation and a vibrant student body that celebrates cultural and socioeconomic diversity. I am eager to take my place on campus and make a positive contribution to the program. America has given me so much; I am eager to give back the fruits of my academic labor.

Our Assessment: This is a commendable essay from a candidate who had accomplished a great deal in a short period of time. By explaining the challenges she faced in a clear and sincere manner, she won the committee's full support.

Addendum to Explain Bad Grades

As the child of an American soldier and Iraqi mother, I was raised by my maternal grandparents in the harsh conditions of post-Gulf War Iraq. At age six, I was diagnosed with rheumatic fever, which required a level of medical intervention that was unavailable in Iraq. My diseased heart grew progressively worse and eventually interfered with my normal activities.

Through the assistance of Doctors without Borders, I came to the United States for medical treatment in 1998. Although the American doctors successfully replaced my mitral valve, my adjustment to the American educational system proved to be as challenging as my medical problems. In addition to my poor English skills, I was unaccustomed to learning in a classroom setting. Throughout my childhood in Iraq, I had been sporadically tutored at home, but I had never attended school. Consequently, I found the formal education system in America to be physically and emotionally overwhelming.

Fortunately, I was up to the challenge. With the help of my father's family, I hired tutors in English, math and reading and quickly raised my grades to an acceptable level. During my sophomore year in college, I maintained a 3.5 GPA, despite serious complications with my valve replacement. After working so hard to assimilate, I refused to let anything stop me from graduating with honors.

Although my GPA isn't the best, I cannot in good conscience blame my illness. After all, the same heart condition that nearly killed me also brought me to my wonderful new life in America. Through painful experience, I have learned to accept life's blessings along with its challenges. My illness brought me closer to my father's family, who welcomed me into their lives. My illness also forced me to rely on an internal compass that I didn't know I had. I developed patience and perseverance by continuing to attend school. I became less focused on my own feelings and more appreciative of others. I also developed a tolerance for change, which, ironically, has been the one constant in my life. Although I have recovered from my disastrous childhood in Iraq, I will retain its many lessons for the rest of my life.

Our Assessment: This essay offers an honest explanation of the candidate's struggles in the classroom. To document his time off from school, the candidate also submitted a letter from the surgeon who replaced his mitral valve. As a result, the committee understood the severity of the candidate's illness and recovery.

Addendum to Explain Bad Grades

My GPA was nearly perfect until I suffered a severe leg injury during my junior year of college. While driving home from my part-time job, I spun out of control on a patch of ice and injured my right leg. In that split second collision, I broke four bones and needed extensive surgery to repair them. I also needed physical therapy to rebuild the damaged tendons.

During my two months in rehab, my focus was on my own recovery rather than my schoolwork. Although I established a good rapport with my tutor, I couldn't concentrate on my assignments. During the first few weeks, I struggled with every minor detail of my hospitalization. I went from being a confident student to a helpless patient who needed help to go to the bathroom. Thanks to the exceptional doctors, nurses and counselors on staff, I managed to get past my initial anger and complete my rehab in just nine weeks.

Unfortunately, the emotional effects of the accident lingered well into my senior year. Because of the residual damage to my leg, I could no longer play football, which had been a huge source of enjoyment and pride. My concentration deficit was also troubling. During the fall semester, I struggled with a heavy course load, including advanced classes in Statics and Electricity. Rather than take a reduced load, I opted to simply do my best and hope that my concentration would improve. Although it eventually did, my GPA paid a heavy price. I hope the admissions committee will understand.

Two professors (Drs. Davis and Hanson), along with my rehab specialist (Dr. White), have provided reference letters to document my struggles after the accident. I offer their letters not as an excuse, but as evidence of the powerful support that I needed to regain my mobility and graduate on time. Several friends and advisors suggested that I take a year off to fully recover. Looking back, that option probably would have enabled me to get better grades, but I am proud to be able to graduate as originally scheduled. The accident was a setback, but not a fatal one. If given a chance, I will bring my dedication and tenacity to all of my endeavors in law school. I am "back in the game" and ready to show you what I can do.

Our Assessment: This candidate shows the reader the *right* way to document an accident that caused a drop in GPA. He told the story quickly and honestly, including his controversial decision to accelerate his workload in order to graduate with his class. Most importantly, he included letters from two faculty members and a physician, who documented his situation in a supportive way. As a result, the committee understood the obstacles the candidate faced to complete his classes and recover from his injuries.

Addendum to Explain a Low GPA

During my junior year of college, my father lost his job as an accountant for United Airlines. Although my mother continued to work as a retail clerk, her salary was not enough to cover our basic living expenses. Within a few months, my parents depleted their savings during my father's unsuccessful job search. Without a miracle, we faced the frightening possibility of losing our family home.

Despite my heavy academic load, I accepted a position as a web designer at Brevard Community College to supplement my mother's income. Balancing a 30-hour work week with a full-time course load was a difficult challenge that left me exhausted and overwhelmed. Sadly, it also diminished my formerly perfect GPA. Despite my best efforts, I did not obtain top grades in my math and science classes, which required considerable outside preparation. On several occasions, I missed our weekly study sessions in order to work enough hours to pay our monthly bills. As a result, my greatest accomplishment is not completing my education, but keeping my family safe and united during this crisis.

My journey, although stressful, has given me the confidence and stamina to pursue my passion for engineering. After tackling this enormous responsibility in a positive manner, I am certain that I can handle the challenges that law school will bring.

<u>Our Assessment</u>: In this short essay, the candidate proved to the committee that he was a survivor. During a tough time, he did what was necessary to help his family and complete his education. By balancing these demands, he developed practical skills that will enhance his performance in law school.

Addendum to Explain a Low LSAT Score

Despite my best efforts, I have been unable to achieve the exceptional LSAT scores that are expected at a school of Yale's caliber. Over the Christmas holidays, I took an extensive LSAT prep course, along with private tutoring sessions with a faculty member. Even with personal coaching, I have been unable to exceed a cumulative score of 149. I am frustrated by these results, because they do not reflect the academic excellence that I have consistently displayed in the classroom.

Despite my difficulty with the LSAT, I am convinced that I am an excellent candidate for your program. Over the past decade, I have developed myriad practical skills that cannot be assessed by standardized testing. I am fluent in four languages and a successful violinist in a professional orchestra. Between 2005 and 2008, I traveled all over the world with the Vienna Boys Choir. Clearly, my LSAT scores do not accurately reflect my fluency in English, proficiency in music, or my unique multi-cultural experiences.

Although I respect your use of the LSAT as a screening tool, I hope that you will consider the "full picture" of my academic, professional and cross-cultural training in making your final admissions decision. I have worked very hard to achieve aggressive professional goals, and I will bring a wealth of practical experience to the classroom. If given the opportunity, I will be a tremendous asset to your program.

<u>Our Assessment</u>: Many students write addendums to explain a disappointing LSAT score. Few have done it better than this candidate, who explained: (1) the efforts he made to obtain a top score and (2) the distinctive strengths that he would bring to law school.

The only controversial part of the essay is his decision to mention his preparation for the LSAT, which included an expensive course and one-on-one tutoring. On one hand, this clearly suggests that the candidate took the test seriously and did whatever he could to prepare for it. On the other hand, it also shows that he had significant financial resources, which some schools consider to be an unfair advantage.

Thankfully, in this case, the candidate's application was otherwise strong, which made the LSAT tutoring and prep course a non-issue. But, from our perspective, this is something that candidates should consider before they disclose that they took an expensive LSAT course. It definitely shows initiative, but it also shows that you have more money than other applicants (who scored well *without* an expensive course). Consequently, it may invite a level of scrutiny that you did not expect.

Addendum to Explain a Low LSAT Score

Like many foreigners who were raised in the United States, I often felt like a fish out of water. My parents moved to the US when I was 14, which subjected me to a huge cultural change that would subsequently define my childhood. My hardest adjustments were with language. Nothing was as difficult as having to learn English with little academic support. The school department in Raleigh had no ESL facilities, so I learned English by working with an old set of Berlitz tapes. It was not easy. My initial attempts at conversation were particularly frustrating. I could visually "see" the word in my mind, but I could not verbalize it. Verb conjugation was a nightmare (sing, sang, sung) as were similar sounding words (to, two, too). Throughout high school and college, mastering English has been my greatest challenge.

Although I have excelled in my coursework, I still have serious difficulties with the language portion of most standardized tests. Consequently, my performance on the verbal portion of the LSAT is not nearly as high as I had hoped. To compensate for this deficiency, I continue to take elective classes in speech and writing; I also volunteer as a language tutor for new students from South America.

As an aspiring attorney, I want to express myself with confidence, both verbally and in writing. I look forward to developing these skills in law school, where I will embrace every opportunity to write papers and speak in front of an audience. I am certain that I will succeed. While navigating the difficult transition from Costa Rica to the US, I developed the confidence to weather even the hardest storms.

Our Assessment: This candidate essentially learned English on her own, which her school principal confirmed in his recommendation letter. As a result, the committee understood the terrible hurdle the candidate faced to score well on standardized tests.

Addendum to Explain a Low LSAT Score

In the spring of 2009, I prepared diligently for the April LSAT, knowing that the results would play a major role in determining where I would obtain my legal education. After months of drills, mock tests and classroom preparation, I was ready to show the Admissions Committee that I could conquer this marathon exam.

Six days before the test, I was rushed to the emergency room at Southland Community Hospital with the most excruciating pain of my life. Lab results showed an inflamed appendix that required immediate removal. Following surgery on April 1 (see attached note from my attending physician), I recovered at the hospital for three days and returned home on Thursday, April 5. Considering my four-inch incision, my doctor recommended complete bed rest for at least five weeks.

With the LSAT scheduled for April 7, I found myself in an unenviable position. Although my surgery was certainly a valid reason for missing the exam, the April testing date was the last one to qualify for 2009 admission. If I missed the April test, my legal education would have been delayed by an entire year. At the time, it seemed like an eternity.

Determined to enroll in law school in the fall of 2010, I refused to miss that test. Against everyone's advice, my brother drove me to the testing site on Saturday morning and waited for me nervously in the car. I could barely stand up, much less concentrate on complex reasoning problems. Nevertheless, I survived the test and even skipped my prescription painkillers that afternoon. I was hurting, exhausted and sore beyond belief, but I completed the test. My final score (154) is respectable, but certainly not what I expected.

As I complete my application, I am fully recovered from my surgery and eager to begin law school. Yet my low LSAT score haunts me, not just because of its mediocrity, but because of the unusual circumstances that surround it. Throughout my college career, I have worked diligently to distinguish myself as a versatile candidate who is highly suited for the legal profession. My grades, work experiences and personal references all support my honorable intentions and goals. Clearly, my LSAT score does not reflect my academic potential, but the extenuating circumstances I faced on the testing day. I hope the committee will consider this as a mitigating factor when they make their admissions decision.

Our Assessment: This candidate told the entire story behind his disappointing LSAT score, which was supported by letters from his physicians. As a result, the committee understood that his score did not reflect his true ability to succeed in law school.

Addendum to Explain a Low LSAT Score

In high school and college, I attained a 3.9 GPA without requesting special accommodations for my learning disabilities (dyslexia and ADHD). By employing effective study techniques, I achieved excellent grades under the same testing conditions as my peers. For philosophical reasons, I chose not to inform my professors or academic advisors of my "special needs" or challenges. Instead, I opted to keep the focus on my talents, rather than my limitations.

Few people supported my position, including my parents and family doctor. In fact, they unanimously agreed that my efforts to compete with "normal" students were doomed to fail. As you might expect, my decision ultimately provided a wonderful sense of empowerment. By thriving academically, I confirmed my ability to succeed in difficult situations, which inspired my commitment to other aspects of personal growth. Contrary to what my guidance counselor told me, there isn't anything I can't do.

In the same vein, I am proud of my "average" LSAT score (145), which I also achieved without special testing accommodations. Although it may not seem particularly impressive, it proves that I can perform at parity with other candidates under extremely stressful circumstances. And to me, that is paramount. After graduation, I will be expected to demonstrate the same skills as my peers. Why not start now?

<u>Our Assessment</u>: For personal reasons, this candidate did not request special accommodations in the classroom or for the LSAT. In this essay, he not only explains that choice, but shows the reader the confident and inspirational person that he is. The essay was well perceived.

Addendum to Explain a Gap in Employment or Education

My parents divorced during my freshman year of high school, which left my mother as the sole support of three small children. As the oldest, I felt a strong responsibility to help her. Just fourteen years old, I got a job as a waitress in a neighborhood diner and contributed my earnings to the household. Between school and work, my schedule left little time for homework, hobbies or extracurricular activities. After a year with virtually no sleep, I realized that I could no longer continue to juggle so many responsibilities.

Sadly, my family's needs had to come first. After withdrawing from high school, I worked full-time at the diner, along with a second job at Variety Print Shop. I took evening classes to prepare for the GED exam, which I passed in October of 2004. After seven long years of night classes, I finally completed my BA in Psychology at the University of Massachusetts-Amherst in 2010. No victory was ever as sweet as walking across the stage to receive my diploma!

As I complete my application for law school, I am painfully aware of how different I am from your traditional applicants. I have nothing to discuss in the sections of the application that ask about hobbies, sports or campus affiliations. My priority was always providing for my family and completing my education; I rarely had the luxury to dream, to follow my passions, or to consider "what if." Compared to more financially secure candidates, I probably sound like a "charity case."

But I prefer the term "winner." At first glance, I haven't had much of an opportunity to demonstrate key leadership skills, yet I have certainly succeeded at building my own life. I persevered in situations in which most people would have given up. I found solutions to difficult problems that seemingly had no answers. I provided for my siblings, to ensure that they would have the chance to find their own success and pursue their own dreams. And I never, EVER complained about the hand that life dealt me, either financially or socially. I am, after all, a self-made woman with the power to transcend seemingly insurmountable challenges. Isn't that what superior leadership is all about?

<u>Our Assessment</u>: This essay is masterful, both in its content and simplicity. The reader clearly understands what the candidate has overcome to complete her education and pursue her dreams.

Addendum to Explain a Gap in Employment or Education

After five years of marriage, I gave birth to my daughter Emily in 2006. Originally, I intended to return to my position at Quaker Oats, Inc., but I had a last minute change of heart. Acknowledging the importance of my baby's first year, I opted to be a stay-at-home mom. Thankfully, my husband's income as a prosecutor was enough to cover our expenses for my one-year sabbatical.

During my time off, I discovered the need for a pregnancy resource center for other young women in the Warren area. Located sixty miles from the nearest major city (San Francisco), local mothers lacked convenient access to counseling, well-baby care, infant and toddler play groups and basic lactation support. I started Madonna & Child Ltd. to address these needs.

Our program provides free and low cost services to all mothers in the Warren/ Barrington area. I raised awareness for the program by making presentations at high schools, college campuses and women's groups in the city. I also solicited donations from local businesses, which were generous with their time, expertise and money. After a slow start, Madonna & Child Ltd. developed a great reputation around the city. After four years of continuous growth, we now have 46 volunteers and over 500 new mothers participating in the program. We provide a comprehensive array of services (GED classes, instruction in baby care, nutrition classes, job hunting skills, and anger management classes) in a supportive, non-judgmental environment.

Although I started Madonna & Child Ltd. as a volunteer resource, it soon became my professional calling. My commitment to the group enables me to enrich the lives of mothers and children in a unique manner. Since 2007, I have served as the company's president and CEO, which requires me to oversee all aspects of the organization's administration and management. After law school, I plan to pursue similar opportunities in the public sector.

Our Assessment: This essay not only explains the candidate's gap in employment, but the unique contribution she has made to her community through the non-profit organization that she launched. It was as persuasive and well-written as her primary statement.

Addendum to Explain a Gap in Employment or Education

Following my junior year of college, I took a one-year sabbatical to assist with a critical public health crisis in my native South Africa. After a three-day riot destroyed Cape Town's impoverished Zenatta Hospital, the government requested that all available medical personnel report for duty. As a registered nurse with Medivac experience, my services were in particularly high demand.

Between August of 2009 and July of 2010, I worked nearly eighty hours per week as a primary care nurse in the Cape Town facility. Because most of the surgical theatres had been destroyed by the riots, I often assisted with surgeries in temporary facilities. Doctors postponed all elective and non-critical procedures, yet we were still overwhelmed by the need for medicine, caregivers and preventive health measures. With few practicing physicians in the community, our emergency room was the only available health care resource.

Throughout my year at the hospital, I heard disparate reports about the causes of the nation's national health crisis. The staff reported widespread misuse of funds, while the national newspaper accused the government of abusing international aid. Whatever the root causes, I found myself in the untenable position of losing patients to potentially curable illnesses because of a lack of money and pharmaceuticals. Sadly, government corruption and media restrictions prevented public appreciation of the issues or the implementation of effective remedies. I was frustrated by my inability to improve the situation.

I returned to college in August of 2010 with a profound skepticism regarding the future of South Africa. As a student of international policy, I have discovered that government secrecy and adherence to the rule of law is not confined to third-world hospitals. Yet my hopelessness in South Africa is occasionally replaced by a newfound confidence. With a strong educated response, along with the skills I will gain from studying in the US, I am confident that I will make meaningful changes in the administration of health care, medical charities and other public aid funds in South Africa.

Our Assessment: This statement is from an older candidate who went back to school to complete her undergraduate degree after working for several years as a nurse. Her detailed account of her emergency "gap year" gives the reader keen insight into her maturity, motivation, and perseverance under difficult circumstances.

Addendum to Explain a Gap in Employment or Education

In the spring semester of my sophomore year at Sarah Lawrence College, my brother died of AIDS. Chris had contracted the disease five years earlier from a tainted unit of blood that he received during emergency surgery. Although my family had known of his diagnosis for years, we were emotionally unprepared for his death. Unable to return to college after Chris's funeral, I wound up taking two years off.

If left to my own devices, I probably would have moped in my room for most of that time. Fortunately, Chris's friends had other ideas. Within a week of his death, his best friend from the local AIDS hospice asked me to participate in a new program designed to promote AIDS awareness in the community. At the first meeting, I realized immediately how much I was needed. The other advocacy groups in town were largely ceremonial in nature; they organized fundraisers, solicited donations and provided financial support for uninsured patients. However, no one was working on the most urgent need, which was education.

I became the official liaison between the group and the local high schools, where we presented free seminars on AIDS prevention. Our first classes were somewhat awkward because I could not discuss sex without embarrassment, but the message was so powerful and important that I never lost my focus. In fact, my youthfulness definitely worked in my favor. At the end of my talks, the kids asked relevant questions about how to "stay safe" in both casual and committed relationships. They helped me to see that I had valuable information to share, even if the topics were intimate and embarrassing.

After returning to Sarah Lawrence in 2009, I continued to teach classes and train new participants in the program. During the past year, I have given speeches on AIDS awareness to both the regional and national

Sigma Tau sorority conferences. Four years after losing Chris, I feel closer to him than ever. I think he would be proud of my work to prevent others from suffering from HIV. My commitment to educating teens is his legacy to me, which I am honored to share with anyone who will listen. With education and awareness, we *will* win this fight.

Our Assessment: The honesty and eloquence of this essay made it far more than simply an "explanation" for the candidate's educational gap. It showed the reader the impact of her brother's death, which inspired her to help prevent the spread of HIV/AIDS in children. After reading it, the committee knew how generous, special, and effective a person she truly was.

Addendum to Explain Arrest / Criminal History

On March 15, 2008, I drove three friends home from our spring break vacation in Daytona Beach, Florida. After nine grueling hours, I didn't realize the magnitude of my fatigue. When I reached the Ohio border, I encountered the worst snowstorm I had ever seen. Although I was tempted to stop at a rest area, I didn't want to delay our arrival. Against my better judgment, I continued driving.

Less than an hour later, I hit a patch of ice and crossed the center line of Route 55, where I hit the driver's side of a Federal Express delivery truck. Fortunately, since both vehicles were traveling at reduced speeds, there were no injuries (other than emotional trauma). Unfortunately, my bad decision had immediate legal repercussions. The Ohio State Trooper cited me for hazardous driving and for failure to maintain control of my vehicle. Three months later, I plead *nolo contendere* at my court appearance in Columbus, Ohio. I received a $500 fine and was ordered to complete a driver education class.

Looking back, I am extremely embarrassed by the incident and my poor judgment. While trying to appear "cool," I caused a horrible accident that jeopardized five young lives. Since that day, I have been an exceptional driver who is reluctant to take chances. I will never make a similar mistake again.

Our Assessment: This essay is short, focused, and sincere. The author also attached a short note from the teacher of his driver education course, who vouched for his maturity and character. As a result, the committee recognized that the incident was not a character defect, but a regrettable error in judgment.

Addendum to Explain Arrest / Criminal History

Two months into my internship with Zenith Computer, the company opted to outsource the manufacturing of our mother boards to a tiny firm in Korea. Although senior management assured us that the company was not a sweatshop that used child labor, I had my doubts. In my previous internship with Wyatt Computer, I had visited a manufacturing plant in the same Korean city where Zenith planned to do business. I saw with my own eyes the age of the workers and the inhumane conditions that they endured. I strongly disagreed with Zenith's decision to support this practice.

Although I was not in a position to change the decision, I presented a videotape of my footage from Korea to a sympathetic manager in human resources. She promised to show it to the senior manager who was in charge of the move. She also asked me to document my concerns in a memo. Unfortunately, my efforts did not alter the firm's decision to outsource the manufacturing function. In late 2007, they proceeded with the move to Korea.

Six months later, when the child labor issue became public knowledge, I led an organized demonstration outside Zenith's Los Angeles headquarters. I was no longer an employee of the firm, simply a concerned citizen who was trying to raise awareness for an atrocious issue. When we refused to voluntarily end our demonstration, Zenith's security team called the Los Angeles Police Department and we were all arrested for disturbing the peace. The charges were eventually dropped when Zenith's legal team failed to appear at a required hearing.

Looking back, I have mixed emotions about leading the demonstration. On one hand, I was honored to publicly challenge a cause as despicable as child labor. On the other hand, a criminal conviction could have handicapped my goal of becoming an attorney. The long-term effect of the arrest was to fuel my determination to change the system by working within it, rather than against it. As a litigator and advocate, I can fight child labor with more effective tools than civil disobedience. Eventually, I hope to be in a position to draft, influence and implement meaningful laws to protect the interests of children across the globe. I can also draw attention to this issue in legal ways that I was not aware of during my internship.

Our Assessment: In this essay, the candidate explained his decision to support an admirable cause in a less than admirable way. The committee was impressed by his passion, honesty, and willingness to put his freedom on the line for his ideals. More importantly, they respected his subsequent decision to pursue a law degree, which would teach him more effective ways to promote social change.

Addendum to Explain Arrest / Criminal History

While driving home from Atlanta's 2006 Fourth of July Parade, I was pulled over during a random DUI screening. Unfortunately, my blood alcohol level was 0.014, which was slightly over the legal limit. I was charged with underage drinking and driving under the influence and was released on my own recognizance. Rather than face the expense of a trial, I plead guilty to the charges in October of 2007. I lost my license for six months, paid a $1500 fine and completed a court-ordered program in drug and alcohol awareness.

During my mandatory classes, I was impressed by the speakers from Students Against Drunk Driving (SADD), including two of my fellow students from UGA. Their frank discussions about alcohol abuse and its devastating effects forced me to reconsider my own personal habits. In my first year of college, I often drank five or six beers on a weekend night and got into my car to drive home. It never occurred to me that I was breaking the law or that my actions could hurt someone else. Although I considered myself a responsible driver, my DUI suggested otherwise.

To my surprise, the speakers were all "nice kids" who had made tragic mistakes while drinking and driving. One girl had caused an accident that killed a young child. After hearing their stories, I realized how foolish and misguided my actions had been. I promised myself that I would never drink and drive again.

After I completed my mandatory classes in drug and alcohol awareness, I joined the UGA chapter of SADD. Two years later, I remain one of its most committed members. By volunteering as a designated driver, I am determined to doing my part to prevent drunk driving.

Our Assessment: This essay explains an unfortunate mistake that many students make- they drink and drive, which can have deadly consequences. In this case, the candidate's record was expunged after he completed his court-ordered drug awareness program. Otherwise, the charges would have remained on his record and prevented him from gaining admission to law school. Along with this addendum, the candidate submitted the actual court record, along with a letter from the judge that stated that he had satisfied all of the terms of his plea agreement. Thankfully, the law school accepted his explanation and granted him admission to their program.

Addendum to Explain Arrest / Criminal History

On my seventeenth birthday, my boyfriend invited me to dinner and a movie at our local shopping mall. While we waited for the show to begin, we took a casual walk through the neighboring stores. Unbeknownst to me, my boyfriend slipped an expensive watch into his pocket while we browsed through a small jewelry shop. When we tried to leave, the security tag on the watch triggered the alarm system and we were immediately surrounded by security guards. We spent the next two hours at the police station, answering some very embarrassing questions.

Although I did not know about the watch, we were both charged with shoplifting and were released to our parents' custody. Ultimately, the store agreed to drop the charges if we would pay for the watch. Needless to say, we apologized profusely to the store manager and paid full retail value for the timepiece.

Although the charges may not appear on my criminal record, the experience changed my life. I faced an evening in jail, along with the embarrassment of having to call my parents. I will never forget the look of shame and disappointment on my mother's face. After spending a lifetime teaching me right from wrong, she never thought that I would steal – or date someone who would. I let her down. I also lost respect for my boyfriend, who was clearly not the honest person I thought he was.

The incident taught me a powerful lesson about the importance of character. Since then, I have been extremely selective in who I choose to befriend. At the same time, I faced the formidable challenge of earning back the respect of my own family. Fortunately, over time, my parents acknowledged that my mistake was not being a thief, but trusting the wrong person. We have subsequently worked very hard to heal as a family.

Our Assessment: In reality, this candidate did not have to disclose this incident, because no charges were filed against her. Nevertheless, the committee respected her for being honest enough to reveal it to them and explain its impact on her life. As part of her application, the candidate reinforced this positive impression by submitting strong recommendation letters that confirmed her personal character.

Addendum to Explain Arrest / Criminal History

On October 11, 1999, I was pulled over by the police and charged with improper lane usage. While inspecting the car, the police found 8 oz. of cannabis, which resulted in an additional charge for possession. On December 1, 1999, the cannabis charge was suppressed; the final disposition was "Motion state stricken on leave to reinstate." On January 4, 2000, I received supervision and a $50 fine for the traffic violation. The case is logged under San Diego Police Dept. - Complaint #9618-93.

Ten years later, I am still embarrassed and humbled by this experience. At age nineteen, I made the mistake of experimenting with something that was illegal and dangerous. I do not use drugs today, nor do I condone their use by others. I deeply regret the pain and embarrassment that my mistake caused my family.

In hindsight, I wish that I had possessed the maturity and insight to have made a better decision. Unfortunately, I made an error in judgment. When evaluating my application, I hope that my committee will consider this incident as an aberration in my otherwise happy, healthy, successful thirty-year life. It was a regrettable mistake that does not in any way reflect the maturity and integrity I will bring to your program.

Before I completed my application to law school, I contacted the State Bar of California to verify that my criminal past would not prohibit me from qualifying for admittance to the state bar. Although they evaluate each case on an individual basis, they assured me that I would have a high probability of success, as long as I meet the following criteria:

1. continue to exhibit fit character now and in the future
2. report the offense honestly on my law school and bar applications
3. show clear and compelling evidence of rehabilitation

My criminal record has been spotless since the incident in 1999. Throughout the subsequent ten years, I have devoted myself to my job, family and community in a positive way. If asked, several business and community leaders are willing to state their support for me. I hope with admissions committee will do the same.

Our Assessment: This author did an excellent job of documenting the incident and apologizing for it. More impressively, he also took the time to verify that he was bar eligible, which few candidates do. The committee was impressed by his solid track record – and ability to put the incident behind him and live a healthy and drug-free life.

Addendum to Explain a Job Loss

In 2007, I became the General Manager for Tropical Gardens, which is a $25 million dollar natural produce business that supplies fresh fruit and organic vegetables to restaurants and food service institutions in northern California. Later that year, I became engaged to the owner's daughter, who coordinated the firm's public relations work. For nearly three years, we worked together in a family business that we hoped to eventually pass on to our children.

Everything changed in the spring of 2010, when my fiancé had second thoughts about our impending marriage. Over a period of three weeks, her "uncertainty" morphed into a realization that she preferred to sever our relationship. I later discovered that her reservations were due to her budding relationship with one of our suppliers. Rather than lead me on, she opted to defer our marriage plans in order to explore another romantic relationship. Needless to say, I was personally and professionally crushed.

To his credit, my fiance's father, who was the president of our firm, never took sides or demanded my resignation. In fact, he continually praised me for doing a commendable job under increasingly stressful circumstances. Nevertheless, I found it impossible to ignore the strained relationships in the office. Eventually, I concluded that such a small company could not thrive if we tried to co-exist together. With mixed emotions, I submitted my resignation in August of 2010 and stayed onboard long enough to train my replacement. Fortunately, a few months later, I located a similar position with Sunkist Foods in San Francisco.

I am grateful for my professional success at Tropical Gardens and for the mature way in which I handled a difficult situation. Sadly, I also learned a painful lesson in not mixing business with pleasure. Whatever the future holds, I will think long and hard before I become romantically involved with a colleague. After my experience at Tropical Gardens, I am extremely reluctant to risk losing another excellent job to the whims of romance.

Our Assessment: Many people find themselves in the same position as this candidate, which forces them to make a difficult professional choice for personal reasons. This essay documented his career transition in a professional and articulate way.

Addendum to Explain a Job Loss

Following my graduation from Columbia University, I accepted a position teaching high school English at a small Baptist school in northern Mississippi. The job was an excellent fit for my degree in education and a unique opportunity to live in a close-knit rural community.

Unfortunately, my liberal religious beliefs were a poor fit for the conservative local diocese. On a regular basis, I received negative feedback for my decision to discuss current events from a secular perspective. From the administration's view, my job was to present the Christian position on each topic and to label all non-Christian influences as negative or destructive. If a student questioned that perspective or asked for my opinion, I was advised to refer them to the Bible. No additional discussion would be permitted.

By the end of my first semester, I felt that I was in an untenable position. The restrictions that were placed on my classroom discussions not only stifled my enjoyment of the job, but my students' ability to learn. By the Christmas holiday season, I felt trapped in my increasingly inhospitable environment. In early spring, the principal informed me that the diocese would not renew my contract for the following school year. Although I hated being fired, I knew that continuing in the job would have been a poor choice for everyone.

Looking back, I accepted the job for all the wrong reasons, without considering the poor interpersonal "fit." As an open-minded woman, I was appalled by the school's inflexible position on topics of moral and social relevance. In my mind, my job was to encourage discussion and nurture independent thinking, not to simply parrot the school's "party line." Fortunately, I quickly landed another teaching position at a public school outside Biloxi. My employers not only tolerated, but supported, my commitment to lively classroom discussions. In fact, I was named "Teacher of the Year" in the Biloxi school district for five consecutive years.

Our Assessment: This candidate did an excellent job of explaining her poor fit for the religious culture at the school where she worked. By writing this essay, she showed considerable insight into her own personality and values, which highly impressed the committee. She also had the opportunity to tell "her side" of a difficult professional situation that one of her recommendation letters also addressed.

Addendum to Explain a Job Loss

I was fired from my position as quality control director for Tommy Hilfiger Ltd. when I defied my supervisor's order to substitute a lower quality fabric for a top retailer. Although the unethical substitution would have saved us nearly six million dollars, it was a clear violation of our original agreement with the buyer. Worse, the difference in quality was noticeable enough to potentially damage our reputation in the marketplace. I refused to go along with the ruse.

Although I was comfortable with my decision to honor my conscience, being a "whistleblower" cost me my job. My boss, who ruled by intimidation and fear, denied my claims and blamed me for the "miscommunication." Considering the disparity in our positions, senior management chose to support my boss. After a brief meeting, I was ordered to vacate the building by the end of the day.

This experience challenged everything I previously understood about teamwork, honesty and doing my best for my company. When senior management refused to back me, I felt that several of my sacred values had been defiled. Sadly, despite his technical strengths, my boss was willing to risk the long-term loss of our brand to achieve a short-term gain. Fortunately, he was fired from the company within a year of the incident, which validated my decision to report his deception. I later discovered that he had made similar substitutions in the past, but that I was the first person to stand up to him. Word of my "insubordination" had slowly trickled into the executive suite and prompted closer scrutiny of the tyrant's unethical practices.

Although my supervisor's undoing came too late to salvage my career at Tommy Hilfiger, it confirmed my commitment to honesty in all aspects of business. Regardless of the temptation to cheat or take shortcuts, I will only be successful if I am willing to be ethically correct and fully accountable for my actions. For the rest of my career, I am determined to be the antithesis of my unethical former boss.

Our Assessment: This candidate paid a heavy price for adhering to her convictions. Nevertheless, she made a positive impression on the admissions committee, who respected her maturity and integrity in a difficult situation.

Addendum to Explain a Job Loss

As an Arab-American woman, I lived for nearly twelve years in the United States without enduring a single act of discrimination. Everything changed after September 11, when fear and mistrust permeated the Yale campus, where I taught classes in International Relations and Policy. In the aftermath of the attacks, I was taunted by profanity and various acts of aggression. One student, with whom I had enjoyed an excellent rapport, actually told me to "burn in hell" when I tried to defend the Muslim religion.

Needless to say, I was horrified by the hostility that was directed toward my Arab friends, students and peers. As an Assistant Professor at the university, I hoped to do my part to confront this anger and prevent other people from being victimized. Unfortunately, my efforts could not stop the misdirected hostility of shell-shocked students. For several weeks, I questioned my decision to remain in the United States.

The point became moot by December, when the university opted not to renew my annual teaching contract. The dean stressed that my performance was not the issue; rather, the situation was a direct result of "decreased interest" in International Relations and Policy classes on campus. Considering the immediate need for soldiers and government workers with a cultural understanding of the Arabic culture and languages, I considered the administration's explanation to be disingenuous. Unfortunately, without tenure, I was in no position to protect my job.

Ironically, losing my faculty position gave me a once-in-a-lifetime chance to serve my country. In January of 2002, through a grant from the State Department, I traveled to the American embassy in Jordan to teach Arabic to thirty US government employees. I was honored to educate others about my native language and culture, and to provide a friendly face during a stressful time. Thankfully, my reception in Jordan was significantly friendlier than that on the Yale campus. My students in Jordan understood that patriots come in all races and wear all styles of clothing. Although I am proud of my Arab heritage, I love being an American and I am committed to preventing further acts of terrorism. I am honored to serve my country in any way possible.

Throughout my year in Jordan, I re-committed myself to a legal career and recovered from the shock of the discrimination I faced in America. When I returned to the United States, I embraced my future with an optimism and clarity I never dreamed possible. As I plan my future and set new goals, I am proud to have made a difference in my own unique way. It was my honor and responsibility as an American.

Our Assessment: This addendum is powerful and eloquent enough to serve as a diversity statement. To the committee, it was a sad reminder of the personal losses that people experienced in the aftermath of September 11, when the emotions of grief-stricken survivors occasionally clouded their judgment.

Addendum to Explain a Job Loss

From 1999 to 2008, I was the co-owner and manager of the Dickinson Chiropractic Group in Atlanta, Georgia. In addition to working with patients, I also developed and implemented the strategic plan for the firm, which served the needs of a heterogeneous population.

Unfortunately, over time, our success was undermined by financial difficulties in the health care industry. As the cost of malpractice insurance skyrocketed, our firm's reimbursement for our services decreased dramatically. In many cases, the amount of reimbursement that we received failed to cover our basic costs of operation. After investing my heart and soul in the practice, I was strangled by crippling loans and little hope for financial relief. Along with other struggling physicians, we closed our office in 2008 and referred our patients to other chiropractors. In addition to leaving me unemployed, this decision ended my dream of providing affordable care in a small office environment.

Closing the practice was a life-altering decision that forced me to look within my soul for spiritual guidance. Although I struggled with a sense of loss and adjustment, I also reconfirmed my professional calling. I am an excellent administrator with a passion for medicine. When I envision my future, I want to use my skills to help other practitioners thrive in an increasingly difficult environment. Part of my motivation to obtain a law degree is to help reform America's health care system. Far too often, qualified physicians are closing their doors because of problems with malpractice insurance and inadequate reimbursement from managed care groups. With legal training, I can find a solution that will be mutually beneficial to both physicians and their patients.

Our Assessment: In his personal statement, this candidate gave an honest explanation for why he decided to change careers after a decade of running his own business. He also cited his interest in promoting health care reform, which was the topic of his personal statement.

Chapter 8: A Second Chance: Responses to Waitlist Notices

Contrary to conventional wisdom, getting into law school isn't a simple "yes or no" proposition. In reality, there are three possible responses to your application: acceptance, rejection or waitlisting. The third category is a frustrating limbo into which thousands of candidates fall each year. What does it mean if you are placed on a waitlist for a top tier law school?

On the positive side, receiving a waitlist letter means that you have qualified for admission. The committee evaluated your application and confirmed that your background and experience are a good fit for their program. But here's where it gets sticky; although they didn't say "no" to your request for admission, they didn't say "yes," either.

Unfortunately, top schools will rarely reveal why a particular candidate is on the waitlist or what (s)he can do to improve his/her chances. Nevertheless, if you are waitlisted at your absolute first-choice school, you have nothing to lose by continuing to market yourself to the Admissions Committee. Unless the school discourages additional contact, we recommend that you take a pro-active approach. Send a letter that restates your interest in the program. Explain the unique contribution that you will make if they admit you.

Keep the letter short and sweet -- two pages maximum. Resist the urge to summarize your life history; instead, stay focused on what you have accomplished since you first applied. Also resist the urge to discuss your disappointment at not being accepted. Your tone must be upbeat and gracious.

This chapter contains three successful letters that candidates submitted in response to being waitlisted. To protect the privacy of the applicants, the names of all people, classes, schools, places, and companies have been changed.

Law School Waitlist Letter

Please accept this letter as my heartfelt intention to remain on the waitlist for admission to the University of Pennsylvania Law School. My recent work as a child advocate has solidified my commitment to the profession and has helped me to better define my long-term goals. Consequently, I am certain that the University of Pennsylvania is the best possible fit for my talents and aspirations.

New Career Developments. Since I originally applied to law school last summer, my career as a psychotherapist has taken an exciting new direction. In late December, I accepted a position as a consultant in the University of Miami Law School's Child Advocacy Legal Clinic. In this capacity, I help inexperienced attorneys develop an understanding of the psychological issues related to child protection, parental termination and foster care. As expected, this work has allowed me to gain an interdisciplinary perspective of the underlying issues relating to child welfare law.

To arbitrate complex family decisions, judges must gather information from diverse sources about a variety of psychological issues, including child development, parental capacities, attachment relationships and family functioning. With my background as a clinical psychologist, I am uniquely qualified to supply and evaluate this information. Over time, my rewarding work for the Child Advocacy Legal Clinic has deepened my interest and involvement in family law.

Future Goals. Although I have grown considerably in my role as a psychotherapist, I often wish that I had the legal background to make a more significant impact on my clients' lives. As I progress in the field, I am drawn to the broader level of change that a law degree will permit me to make. My long-term objective is to integrate my background in psychology and the law to enhance the lives of children and families. As an African-American female, I feel particularly invested in the plight of poor and minority children who are over-represented in the child welfare system. The decisions made in the courtroom have a bottom-line impact on these children's entire lives; thus, it is vitally important that their needs be properly assessed and considered at all stages of intervention. After I obtain my JD, I plan to play a key role in developing viable legal and psychological strategies to assist them.

Why the University of Pennsylvania? As a native of Philadelphia, I feel a strong responsibility to give back to the community that carefully nurtured me through a very difficult childhood. At age two, when my birth mother abandoned me, I found myself at the mercy of an overwhelmed and disorganized social service system. Without the assistance of a caring child advocate, I might never have found the loving foster family that gave me the gift of an education. Clearly, I am compelled to share my blessings with other innocent children who face similar physical, financial and emotional struggles. Attending law school in Philadelphia will allow me to offer pro bono counseling services at Kristy's House, which is a non-profit group that provides free and low cost legal services to families in need.

The University of Pennsylvania Law School has an unparalleled reputation for its groundbreaking work in family law. I am particularly eager to take classes with recognized experts in child advocacy, including Professor Carl Knowlton, who litigated the landmark case of emancipated minors in 1974. Experts like Dr. Knowton and Dr. Clarise Givens, who served as my thesis advisor for my Master's Degree in 2006, will provide the proper balance of legal and psychological theory to support my future goals. At this stage of my career, I am seeking an academic environment that emphasizes not just the practical elements of law, but also the philosophical, contextual, and social dimensions of jurisprudence. The University of Pennsylvania Law School is nationally recognized for providing this kind of dynamic learning environment.

My Fit for Your Program. My life experiences, breadth of knowledge, and commitment to public service will allow me to contribute greatly to the diversity and strength of the University of Pennsylvania student body. They have also given me the intellectual capacity, perseverance, and maturity I will need to champion the rights of children.

As a family and child therapist, I have counseled numerous people whose lives have been profoundly impacted by events in the courtroom. Whether working with victims of domestic violence, child abuse, divorce or contested custody, I have learned a great deal from observing and participating in the legal process. I cannot imagine a better place to enhance my skills than at the University of Pennsylvania.

Our Assessment: This is an exceptional letter from an exceptional candidate who had her heart set on completing her law degree at Penn. This persuasive letter helped her to open that door.

Law School Waitlist Letter

I was recently placed on the waitlist for Fall 2011 admission to the University of Michigan Law School. Unfortunately, due to my current position in Anchorage, Alaska, I was not able to visit the campus to meet with a member of the admissions committee. Consequently, I did not have the opportunity to discuss recent aspects of my application that reflect my ability to succeed in the profession, including:

a. As an engineer at IBM, I single-handedly solved a pressing problem on the XXX chip, which expedited its commercialization. This exciting new technology, which has allowed the company to penetrate the lucrative communications market, has already delivered $55 million to IBM's bottom line. In the next five years, it is expected to generate more than $34 billion dollars in profit on a global basis by leveraging our existing technologies. By serving as the "point person" for all XXX commercialization activities, I demonstrated my flair for development and my ability to be an agent for change in the organization.

b. I received a corporate award for my contribution to Project YYY, which was the largest embedded memory ever designed at IBM. Due to pre-existing design and personnel issues, this project was easily the most challenging and invaluable experience of my professional career. By clearly defining our goals and objectives, I challenged my team members to deliver their personal best under stressful circumstances. The subsequent benefits of our success, including our resulting confidence and camaraderie, continue to be a great source of personal pride.

c. While representing my local chapter of Toastmasters, I won first place in the West Coast Speaking Championship. I was subsequently invited to deliver my speech on rural home businesses at the Alaska Governor's Ball in April of 2011.

d. I received a Certificate of Appreciation from Senator Lisa Murkowski for my fundraising efforts on behalf of Amnesty International.

I appreciate the opportunity to share these achievements with the admissions committee, because they document my ability to pursue a career in technology law. Over the past several years, I have aggressively pursued a series of challenging personal and professional assignments to prepare myself for law school. If given the opportunity, I will bring the same determination to my studies at the University of Michigan. Because of its unparalleled reputation in the academic community, particularly in the area of technology law, Michigan is my first choice for my legal education; if granted admission, I will eagerly accept a seat in the class.

Please contact me at (phone number) or (email address) if you require additional information.

Our Assessment: This letter, although long and technical, drove home several points that the candidate had failed to include in his personal statement, including his passion for technology law and his specific interest in the University of Michigan. The letter also showed his excellent writing skills, which made a positive impression on the committee.

Law School Waitlist Letter

Despite being placed on the waiting list at Harvard Law School, I am convinced that the program is the ideal place for me to obtain my legal education. Please accept this letter as my intention to enroll if space becomes available in the class.

Aristotle taught us that the path to success involves a constant dialogue between hardship and joy, family and career. Over the past year, my experiences have confirmed his teachings. My joy and sense of accomplishment include:

1. graduating Summa Cum Laude from the University of San Diego (at age 46) with a dual degree in history and social services

2. paying my own way through college and graduating with zero debt

3. continuing my rewarding work as a volunteer tutor for learning disabled children at San Marcos Elementary School, where I help students navigate their way through young adulthood

4. being named 2011's "Volunteer of the Year" for the state of California, and accepting the award from Governor Arnold Schwarzenegger at a ceremony in Sacramento

In contrast, the past year has also brought great hardship, as I lost both of my parents to cancer and faced the emotional strain of selling our family home. My grief, fortunately, was abated by the support of my three adult children and my recent academic and community achievements, which represent the culmination of a lifetime of hard work and dedication. After waiting several decades to pursue my legal aspirations, I approach the law school experience with a profound sense of gratitude and optimism.

As I look to the future, I am eager to augment my skills as a social worker with a law degree to make a more meaningful contribution to my community. As a first step, I recently accepted a position as the Interim Director at the San Marcos Center for Children, which is a research and evaluation agency associated with the University of San Diego that fosters youth development through collaborative efforts. This six-month position will end just before law school starts in September. During this time, I will develop a strategy to enable our corporate sponsors to implement their expansive vision. My time at the center will also provide first-hand exposure to child and family law, which an area in which I have more than twenty years of professional experience.

Before I completed my application to Harvard Law School, I spoke with professors Harold Greene and Sondra Wyatt, who strongly encouraged me to apply. After working with me for several years on the Board of Directors for the San Mateo County Child Protective Agency, they felt that my talents and skills were an excellent fit for your program. I am intrigued by the possibilities that Harvard Law School will offer me, including the chance to use my skills as a social worker at the Bernard Koteen Office of Public Interest Advising.

With the support of your dedicated faculty, I am certain that Harvard will provide a legal education of the highest caliber to prepare for a life of public service. If admitted, I will do everything possible to make a lasting contribution to the HLS community.

Our Assessment: Many waitlisted candidates contact the school to update their file, but few do it as powerfully as this applicant, who shed new light on her credentials in this simple, honest, and straightforward letter. The committee knew that she would add considerable strength, intelligence, and diversity to their program.

Chapter 9: Final Thoughts

After reading this book, we hope that you feel well-prepared to write your own persuasive law school personal statement. For best results:

1. Answer the question that was asked.
2. Write naturally, but concisely.
3. Use excellent grammar and punctuation.
4. Show your real personality (let the reader get to know you).
5. Only use humor if it works.
7. Convey a positive message (avoid cynicism).
8. Use the active voice.
9. Be specific and focused / explain events whenever appropriate.
10. Revise and polish until it is perfect.

For additional help in writing and editing letters of recommendation, admissions essays, and personal statements, please visit www.ivyleagueadmission.com.

Remember: in the law school admissions process, personal statements can provide the committee with information about your character, motivation and goals that they could not acquire any other way. A well-crafted essay can also explain a variety of personal circumstances (and obstacles) that have affected your performance. By writing a persuasive essay, you will increase your chances of gaining admission to the law school of your dreams. Don't miss this chance to claim your destiny!

www.ingramcontent.com/pod-product-compliance
Lightning Source LLC
Chambersburg PA
CBHW080252170426
43192CB00014BA/2654